General editor: Graham Handley MA PhD

Brodie's Notes on Thomas Middleton's
and William Rowley's

The Changeling

Peter Washington MA B Litt
Senior Tutor and Deputy Head, The Graduate Diploma, Middlesex Polytechnic

Pan Books London and Sydney

First published 1986 by Pan Books Ltd
Cavaye Place, London SW10 9PG
9 8 7 6 5 4 3 2 1
© Pan Books Ltd 1986
ISBN 0 330 50215 8
Photoset by Parker Typesetting Service, Leicester
Printed and bound in Great Britain by
Richard Clay (The Chaucer Press) Ltd, Bungay, Suffolk

Contents

References in these Notes are to the Penguin English Library
edition of *Three Jacobean Tragedies*, edited by Gāmini Salgādo but
the Notes may be used with any edition of the play.

Preface

The intention throughout this study aid is to stimulate and guide, to encourage the reader's *involvement* in the text, to develop disciplined critical responses and a sure understanding of the main details in the chosen text.

Brodie's Notes provide a summary of the plot of the play or novel followed by act, scene or chapter summaries, each of which will have an accompanying critical commentary designed to underline the most important literary and factual details. Textual notes will be explanatory or critical (sometimes both), defining what is difficult or obscure on the one hand, or stressing points of character, style or plot on the other. Revision questions will be set on each act or group of chapters to test the student's careful application to the text of the prescribed book.

The second section of each of these study aids will consist of a critical examination of the author's art. This will cover such major elements as characterization, style, structure, setting, theme(s) or any other aspect of the book which the editor considers needs close study. The paramount aim is to send the student back to the text. Each study aid will include a series of general questions which require a detailed knowledge of the set book; the first of these questions will have notes by the editor of what *might* be included in a written answer. A short list of books considered useful as background reading for the student will be provided at the end.

Graham Handley

Literary terms used in these notes

conceit A fanciful image or startling comparison. A favourite form of 17th-century metaphor.

irony Saying the opposite of what is meant.

dramatic irony This occurs when a character is unaware of the true significance of his words or actions but other characters on stage, as well as the reader and the audience, know exactly what is happening.

metonymy The substitution of an attribute for a thing, i.e. *crown* for *king*.

oxymoron Opposites combined in one expression, e.g. *bitter-sweet*.

The writers and their work

Born in 1580, Middleton belonged to the Elizabethan middle classes; his father was a prosperous merchant. After attending Oxford the young Middleton married into a distinguished intellectual and literary family. He began publishing as early as 1597 (a long moral poem, *The Wisdom of Solomon Paraphrased*) and continued to write prolifically until his death in 1627, becoming in the meantime Chronologer to the City of London, a post which involved writing speeches, providing public entertainments and compiling a journal of public events.

Middleton's early plays are mostly 'citizen comedies' – popular satirical works aimed at the wider London audience. This type of entertainment was especially common in the first decade of the seventeenth century, when Jonson and Marston were both producing fine examples. In the next decade Middleton followed the changing fashion for tragi-comedy, led by Beaumont and Fletcher. It was in his last years that he turned to the production of tragedies – notably *The Changeling* (1622) and *Women Beware Women* (1621) – though his last fine play, *A Game At Chess* (1624) returns to the satirical mode. This should caution us against the tendency to divide his work into the traditional three phases: early, middle and late, with all the implications such a division has for grandiose theories about a writer's development. Middleton's work is distinguished by its professionalism and its eye for the market place. He wrote his plays for actors and audiences, and largely lacks the intellectual appeal of Shakespeare, Webster and Jonson. This is not to disparage Middleton's work, merely to suggest that its considerable power is best understood when considered in its proper context, the popular theatre.

This last point applies even more to Rowley, who had been a professional actor for many years before he collaborated with Middleton, and remained so until the end of his life, as far as we know. Though Rowley probably died in the mid-1620s, the date of his birth is unknown. He first appears in history as a member of the Duke of York's company of actors in 1608, so he may be roughly contemporary with Middleton, or slightly younger. Like his collaborator, he wrote in non-dramatic forms, though his main work was in the theatre. Scholars have identified up to fifty plays in which they detect Rowley's hand, but only four of these appear to be by him alone – and none have held the stage. He worked with Webster, Dekker, Ford, Fletcher, Heywood, Massinger and others, and appears to have collaborated with Middleton on several plays between 1615 and 1623. On the stage Rowley had a decided talent for comic parts, and the comic writing in *The Changeling* is attributed to him. However, like most Jacobean writers, he was versatile: he wrote elegies and pamphlets and contributed to serious scenes in *The Changeling* and elsewhere.

The Changeling

Plot

Beatrice-Joanna is betrothed to Alonzo de Piracquo, but a few days before the wedding she meets Alsemero and they fall violently in love. Alsemero's friend Jasperino is astonished by this change in one who has previously taken no interest in women. It turns out, however, that Alsemero is the son of an old friend of Vermandero, Beatrice's father. He is made welcome to Vermandero's castle. In the meantime Antonio and Franciscus, two of Vermandero's courtiers, take up residence in the asylum run by Alibius, pretending to be deranged. We later learn that they are both in pursuit of Alibius's attractive wife Isabella.

Beatrice continues her covert flirtation with Alsemero, who offers to challenge Alonzo to a duel so that they may dispose of him and marry each other. Beatrice rejects this idea as too dangerous, but realizes that the man who could dispose of Alonzo is De Flores, a hideous servant of her father's whom she has always hated, but who is devoted to her. As soon as Beatrice looks kindly on De Flores and hints at what she wants, he eagerly offers to kill Alonzo, expecting that she will reward him with her love. Beatrice, however, is counting on De Flores's guilt to make him flee the country, thus ridding her of two disliked men with one blow: Alonzo and De Flores himself. She persuades her father to ask for a short postponement of the marriage; Alonzo agrees, but his brother Tomazo suspects that Beatrice is indifferent to Alonzo.

Charged with showing Alonzo round Vermandero's castle, De Flores has a good opportunity to kill him and dispose of the body, after cutting off a finger to steal a diamond ring that Beatrice had given to Alonzo. Franciscus and Antonio meanwhile make their advances to Isabella but she rejects them; they are observed by Lollio, Alibius's servant who helps him run the asylum.

De Flores demands payment from Beatrice: nothing less than her own body will do, and he is angry when she offers him money. In the end she agrees to let him make love to her. This causes a problem when, in the absence of Alonzo, who has apparently fled, Vermandero agrees to Beatrice's marriage with

Alsemero. Alsemero is bound to realize on the wedding night that Beatrice is not a virgin. Moreover, Beatrice discovers that Alsemero has a potion which, when taken by a woman, infallibly reveals whether or not she is a virgin. In desperation she induces her maid Diaphanta to try the potion and finds that Diaphanta does indeed manifest the symptoms of virginity described in Alonzo's book. She also persuades Diaphanta to take her place in the marriage-bed on the first night after the wedding: in the dark Alsemero will take her for Beatrice and believe his wife to be a virgin. When Alsemero, alerted by Jasperino's suspicions of a conversation he and Diaphanta have overheard between De Flores and Beatrice, tries his potion on Beatrice, she is able to simulate the symptoms it produced in Diaphanta. He is satisfied and angrily rejects Jasperino's hint that De Flores and Beatrice are lovers; the marriage goes ahead. When Tomazo, Alonzo's brother, voices his suspicion that Alonzo has been murdered, Vermandero promises action but does not think of investigating Beatrice or her new husband.

To celebrate the wedding Vermandero requests Alibius to provide an entertainment with the inmates of his asylum. Alibius instructs Lollio to prepare them. Lollio and Isabella also devise a plan to trick Antonio and Franciscus. Isabella dresses up as a madwoman and frightens Antonio, then reveals herself and shows her contempt for him; Lollio lets Franciscus know that his plan is discovered. But Lollio also tells both Antonio and Franciscus separately that Isabella will accept whichever one disposes of the other. Each resolves to frighten away his rival.

On the wedding night Beatrice waits anxiously for Diaphanta to leave the marriage-bed, so that she herself may slip in beside Alsemero. When Diaphanta has not arrived by 3 a.m., Beatrice and De Flores decide to act. De Flores will start a fire in Diaphanta's room, then raise the alarm. When Diaphanta comes rushing back to her room, De Flores will kill her with a gun loaded on the pretext that he is going to clear the chimney by shooting up it. In the confusion no one will realize what is happening and Beatrice may return to bed with Alsemero afterwards. The plan works: Diaphanta is killed and her body burnt. The blame for the fire is put upon her own carelessness. Beatrice artfully distances herself from De Flores by encouraging the others to reward him. But while they are carrying out their plan, the ghost of Alonzo appears to De Flores and to Beatrice, who is terrified by the omen.

Tomazo, filled with suspicion, resolves to abandon the company of men until he discovers his brother's murderer. While meditating on this he is passed by de Flores, to whom he takes a sudden and violent hatred. The two men exchange blows and De Flores believes that Tomazo instinctively knows that he is Alonzo's murderer. At this point, however, Vermandero arrives, explaining that he has solved the mystery: two of his own courtiers, Franciscus and Antonio, had disappeared on the very day of the murder, and are no doubt responsible. Tomazo agrees to interrogate them. Alsemero and Jasperino enter. They have seen Beatrice and De Flores together in the garden, and Alsemero now believes Jasperino's accusations: De Flores is Beatrice's lover. Beatrice enters and is immediately challenged by her husband. She denies the charge, but in order to demonstrate her devotion to Alsemero admits to her part in the murder of Alonzo, saying that she employed De Flores to do the deed – which explains her connection with him. Horrified, Alsemero pushes her into the next room. When De Flores enters, he taxes him with the murder and De Flores at once admits to it. He is ordered into the same room with Beatrice.

When Vermandero and Tomazo enter with the alleged culprits, Franciscus and Antonio (plus Alibius, Lollio and Isabella), Alsemero tells them who the real murderers are. Cries are then heard from within the room, and De Flores is brought out with the wounded Beatrice. After admitting the truth, De Flores stabs himself. He then dies and so does Beatrice. Tomazo acknowledges that justice has been done, Franciscus and Antonio vow to behave foolishly no longer, and Alibius agrees to behave more sensibly towards his wife. It is left to Alsemero to deliver the epilogue.

Sources and treatment

There seem to be three sources for the plot of *The Changeling*. The most important is the floridly titled *The Triumphs of God's Revenge against the Crying and Execrable Sin of Wilfull and Premeditated Murder* by John Reynolds. This work, published a year before the play's first production is a collection of narratives, like many of the source-books for Elizabethan and Jacobean drama; and *The Changeling* is based on the fourth story of the thirty. In *his* narrative Reynolds divides the story of Beatrice, De Flores and Alsemero into three parts. First, Beatrice and Alsemero meet in the church and fall in love; Beatrice arranges for De Flores to murder her betrothed, Alonzo; and she and Alsemero are married. Then Alsemero, for no apparent reason, becomes violently jealous of Beatrice, and she, in turn, begins to hate him, becoming the mistress of De Flores. Alsemero catches and kills them. In the last section Alonzo's brother Tomazo challenges Alsemero, who uses trickery to kill him. Alsemero then tries to escape but is captured and executed. For Reynolds all this serves as an opportunity to moralize: he shows little flair for the dramatic and a curious neglect of motive. No reason is given for Alsemero's jealousy of Beatrice or for his duel with Tomazo, and all the characters are wooden. Reynolds's purpose – as the pompous title of his book indicates – is to illustrate the punishment of sin and the necessity of obedience to God's will. In the process he is able to insinuate a good deal of prurient material about adultery, no doubt designed to increase his readership. The combination of sex, violence and crude morality was as popular then as it is now.

While they adopted the basic outline of this plot, *Middleton and Rowley made major changes to it* – most strikingly in character and motivation. De Flores is transformed from a 'Gallant young Gentleman' in Reynolds, into a hideous amoralist, prepared for any wickedness to satisfy his desires. Alsemero becomes brave and honourable; and Beatrice takes on a depth and subtlety of character quite lacking in the original. The move from moral caricature to complex character results in greater credibility and consistency of motive. Alsemero's irrational jealousy is replaced by an infatuated faith in his wife which only gradually gives place to the evidence of his friend and of his own eyes. The duel with Tomazo is displaced by the dénouement in which the true murderers are revealed. Above all, the change in De Flores makes possible the extraordinary psychological study of Beatrice's reactions to him: loathing, followed by disdainful employment, admiration, and even love. The way in which the heroine turns from positive hatred to an acceptance that her dreadful fate is linked with De Flores is all the more remarkable because, on the face of it, this seems less likely than the original narrative – in which De Flores is attractive. But the gift the authors show for morbid psychology and dramatic intensity is what lifts them far above the level of Reynolds's flaccid moralizing.

In *The Changeling* morality is not simply a matter of melodramatic divine vengeance striking down individuals but a subtle web in which the very being of the characters is involved, a consciousness of good and evil, which either permeates their behaviour (as in the case of De Flores), or which is brought horribly and logically home to them in the consequences of their own actions (as with Beatrice). Like Iago, De Flores knows that what he does is wrong, and almost revels in the knowledge, whereas Beatrice is blind to the significance of her desires and the actions they provoke until it is too late. This central character-contrast is typical of the skill the authors apply to the crude material provided by Reynolds.

However, much of the play's material, especially in the second half, owes nothing to the blood and thunder of the primary source, and it seems that a book published in the same year as *The Changeling* (1622) had something to do with its genesis. *Gerardo, The Unfortunate Spaniard* is a translation from the Spanish of G. de Cespedes y Meneses by one Leonard Digges. In this story the heroine, Isdaura, is left by her father in the care of an old servant. When the father returns and decides to marry his daughter to Roberto, the son of a friend, the servant is bitter, for he had hoped to marry Isdaura himself. He goes to her room one night, confesses his love, and threatens to kill her. Terrified, she promises her hand to him, and he is so overcome by passion that he rapes her. Later she kills him, and gets away with it; but on her wedding night she has to substitute a virgin in Roberto's bed in order to conceal the fact that she is no longer a maid. The parallels with Middleton and Rowley are clear: Alsemero is the son of Vermandero's old friend; he is displaced in his wife's affections by a servant; she substitutes a virgin in his bed on the wedding night. Beyond these similarities, the evidence for borrowing is vague, and the dates of entry in the *Stationers' Register* (March and May 1622) suggest a very hurried reading of the source – though this is not unlikely for the time. Moreover, the various elements of the plot can all be found elsewhere. However, close comparison of Acts IV and V of *The Changeling* with Digges's translation do suggest that it was used as a source. If it was, that provides another example of the dramatists' skill, for they have used the material to far more powerful effect. The character of De Flores, which touches the servant in Digges at several points, is altogether more brilliant and complex; he and Beatrice raise the action from the level of melodrama to high tragedy.

The third source for Middleton and Rowley was their own previous work. Both were experienced dramatists who had previously used several of the situations in *The Changeling*. Rowley, for example, used the murdered substitute in his *All's Lost By Lust* and Middleton had already developed a version of the scene in which De Flores demands his full reward from Beatrice in *A Fair Quarrel*. One might cite other instances of this practice, and also point to similarities with other dramatists. Both Middleton and Rowley collaborated with other writers, and there was a common stock of material in the early seventeenth century, on which everyone drew. This becomes clear when we look at the comic sub-plot, which is based on themes ubiquitous in the period: the old husband and the young wife; the knowing servant; the disguised imposters; the madhouse – can all be found in every playwright from Shakespeare to the Restoration. Rowley was especially adept at manipulating this sort of material, and he is believed to be largely responsible for the sub-plot. But even Middleton – a more distinguished serious dramatist than Rowley – had earlier written *The Family of Love*, in which two rivals gain entrance to the house of a doctor with the aim of seducing his wife: to do so they pretend to be patients, but the doctor outwits them. The sub-plot in itself is neither distinguished nor valuable: the humour is coarse and the action trivial. What matters is its relation to the main plot and the light it throws on that. In order to discuss this relationship we need to consider the question of collaboration.

Collaboration

This was a common practice in the early seventeenth century. Among playwrights Dekker, Webster, Massinger, Beaumont, Fletcher, Jonson, Shakespeare, Middleton and Rowley all worked together in various combinations – often impossible to disentangle now. The theatre was a major popular entertainment and one of the few ways in which a professional writer could make a living. Many dramatists, like Shakespeare, were themselves actors. They were used to working under difficult conditions, and knew that they had to please their audiences in order to survive. Collaboration was a means of increasing productivity and popular appeal. It meant that each writer could concentrate on what he was good at, and that these efforts could then be pooled to maximum effect. This was not always successful. Multiple authorship often leads to confusion and even incoherence in the plays, which sometimes reach a lowest common denominator of weak comedy and crude sensationalism in the bid for popularity – especially in the word of the later Jacobean dramatists. One might compare the trashier output of Hollywood, aimed at the most lucrative public with the coarsest taste. *The Changeling*, for all its weaknesses, is well above this level, partly because the collaboration appears to have been unusually close: there are no obvious contradictions or muddles in the play, which works smoothly and logically, making a clear connection between its two elements: the comic and the tragic. While it doesn't avoid broad effects and esoteric tricks – such as the virgin-testing potion – these are all justifiable in the context.

As it happens, scholars are largely agreed, on the basis of textual evidence, that the two playwrights divided the writing between them on one very simple principle: Rowley wrote most of the comedy and Middleton most of the tragedy. Allowing for disagreement about detail, the division of labour looks something like this:

I,1; I,2	Rowley
II,1; II,2	Middleton
III,1; III,2	Middleton
III,3	Rowley
III,4	Middleton
IV,1; IV,2	Middleton
IV,3	Rowley
V,1; V,2	Middleton
V,3	Rowley

Broadly speaking, this division suggests that Rowley was responsible for the sub-plot and the play's beginning, but that he also contributed to the tragic parts of the drama. Middleton was responsible for the scenes in which the central relationships were developed – particularly II,2 and III,4, in which Beatrice and De Flores develop their relationship. The play's most thorough editor, N. W. Bawcutt (see 'Further reading', p.88), suggests that Rowley belongs with such popular dramatists of the period as Dekker and Heywood, while Middleton had a subtler and more sophisticated mind, which puts him closer to Webster and Jonson. It is certainly true that Middleton's later work bears out this assessment of him. The main point is that between them the two authors produced a unified and coherent drama, and that is the measure of their success.

Scene summaries, critical commentaries, textual notes and revision questions

Act I Scene 1

Alsemero postpones his return to Valencia from Alicante because he has seen the beautiful Beatrice in church and fallen violently in love with her. His friend Jasperino is astonished by this: Alsemero has never fallen for a woman before. But when Beatrice appears, it transpires that she, too, is in love – with Alsemero. De Flores, whom she angrily repulses, announces the arrival of her father Vermandero, who greets Alsemero as the son of an old friend. Beatrice, already betrothed to Alonzo, tries to persuade her father to postpone the wedding a little, on the plea that she is not yet ready to give up her virginity. He ignores this, but invites Alsemero to visit his castle. Meanwhile Jasperino and Diaphanta, Beatrice's maid, strike up a flirtation. The scene ends with Beatrice's angry rejection of De Flores's help, and his vow that he will pursue her whatever she says; for he, too, is in love.

Commentary

There is nothing particular in this scene to suggest tragedy; we might very well be preparing for a comedy. The crudely drawn passions, the humorous by-play of the servants, the love interest, the beautiful daughter, overbearing father and discontented servant – these are all the materials of comedy from classical times. There are, however, one or two signs that this is not to be a comedy. The violence and irrationality of emotions are both marked: Beatrice seems to have an extraordinary effect on men. Alsemero senses that all is not well; Jasperino notes that he is acting out of character; Beatrice and De Flores both experience pain and frustration in their different ways – and the whole atmosphere of this first scene is slightly strained. What impresses the spectator is the claustrophobic sense of obsession which begins to envelop the leading characters from the outset. There is nothing gentle about the love these characters feel for one another: it is close to hate De Flores's closing words – 'I'll have my will' – and the intensity of his tone should alert us to the seriousness of what is to follow, if nothing else does.

The first scene establishes the central relationships with great clarity: Alsemero and Beatrice, Vermandero and Beatrice and, above all, De Flores and Beatrice. As the last sentence suggests, it also makes very clear the way in which the whole action revolves round Beatrice: her beauty, her sexuality, her quick, violent, sensuous temperament. The authors are not especially interested in the setting, the social milieu, the historical context or the minor characters, though all play a peripheral role. What matters is desire: Alsemero's for Beatrice, hers for him, and De Flores's for her.

temple Church.
same i.e. the same girl in the same place.
Follows of Follows from.
Why ... timorous? In view of what ensues, this question becomes retrospectively ironic. So does the following line.
holy purpose Marriage. But, as Alsemero is to discover, a holy purpose can be achieved by evil means.
the place blest Eden. The complicated syntax of this sentence obscures the sense: Alsemero compares the temple to Eden and Joanna and himself to Adam and Eve.
back Again.
it Marriage. Alsemero's idealistic view is firmly established, to contrast with what follows.
join ... one Make us man and wife.
beginning and perfection i.e. the beginning of complete (paradisal) happiness.
buy a gale It was commonly believed that witches controlled and sold winds.
a'God's name In God's name, i.e. free.
The temple's vane In line 2 Alsemero spoke of omens: for the audience this is an unfavourable one.
well ... well Note the play on words – also that illness is a recurrent image.
hidden malady Again ironic. The sickness is worse than he suspects.
doubt Fear.
any cause This suggests the strength of Alsemero's passion.
trap Fit up.
for the speed To make haste.
with'em With the sailors.
orisons Prayers.
church Alsemero's words refer us back to the opening lines. In fact, he *has* changed his 'faith' – to love of Beatrice.
Lover Again ironic – again emphasizing the enormous change which has taken place.

Stoic i.e. someone professedly indifferent to pleasure or pain.

violent The notion of 'violent' passion and the violence it produces is often referred to in the play.

a-going In the process of getting ready.

Backwards Jasperino is characteristically dry and humorous.

critical Propitious.

the sign in Aquarius In the Zodiac, Aquarius is an air sign, and propitious for travelling.

smoke...fire A reference to Alsemero's smouldering passions.

I do not...sea Again ironic: he speaks truer than he knows.

Ere Before.

e'en Even; here meaning 'by all means'.

laws of the Medes A reference to the Old Testament (Daniel, 6,12); proverbially unalterable.

in my conscience I'm absolutely sure.

ne'er Never.

Valencia Alsemero's home town.

ransomed...Turk Greece was then under the control of the Turks.

weak Bad.

Our eyes...blind The evidence of our eyes should lead us to judge well. Sometimes we are led astray by what we see until our better judgment corrects us. The verbal play of Beatrice's speech and Alsemero's reply is heavy handed. The rhyming couplets are awkward and the elaboration out of proportion to the ideas.

further More advanced – both in love and in wit.

Yesterday i.e. when he first saw Beatrice.

Was...employment Did I see you.

hither i.e. to this conclusion.

Both houses The reference is to the Houses of Parliament: both must agree for a bill to become law. Beatrice continues the constitutional metaphor.

one above me i.e. her father, who is above her as God is above the sovereign who gives assent to laws.

For five days past Beatrice has been engaged for five days.

meant i.e. by Fate.

So near his time Because Beatrice's marriage is fast approaching; Alsemero should have been the groom.

by the carriers By the luggage vehicle, i.e. by land.

sea-provision A pun on (i) provisions consumed at sea, (ii) the effort to travel by sea.

at farthest Hugely off course: Jasperino speaks metaphorically.

I'll board her Has the subordinate meaning of 'make love to'.

lawful prize Captured enemy ships were subject to plunder by the captors.

Is in health Beatrice's sharp interruption indicates her irritation at De Flores's presence.

Your eye De Flores takes up the eye-imagery of lines 73–89. It is associated especially with Beatrice.

What needed Why did it need?
One side nor other? One way or another.
enjoined Compelled – by his own desire.
a peevish will Contrariness. The violent irritationality of Beatrice's
  emotions is central to the story.
Than his or hers Than this or that. She means she cannot give a
  reason.
They i.e. the 'him or her' referred to in the previous line.
Such ... basilisk He has on me the effect the basilisk is said to have.
basilisk A mythical creature which killed with its glance.
frailty Weakness.
nature Human nature.
distastes Dislikes.
infinites Many others.
enemy of poison i.e. antidote.
this fault i.e. irrational dislike.
your poison It is ironic that Beatrice should ask this question: she
  herself turns out to be Alsemero's 'poison'.
My memory has I can remember.
want Lack means.
out of his place Meaning both 'not doing his proper job' (attending
  Vermandero), also 'where he shouldn't be'.
mad Jasperino plays on the senses of 'insane' and 'wild'.
physic Medicine.
state Diaphanta alludes to the common comparison between the body
  and a country: both governed by the head. Taking up Jasperino's
  banter she implies his head is weak.
compound Mix. The 'thing' Jasperino refers to is his penis.
poppy Opium.
pop Kiss.
simple Medicinal herb.
cuckoo Wild arum – but also a euphemism for penis.
show thee all Again a double entendre. This conversation is a coarse
  parody of Alsemero's talk with Beatrice.
devotion Prayer. But there is a double meaning: he has interrupted
  her 'prayer' to Alsemero.
my saint Beatrice takes up her father's remark. In the 16th-century
  Roman Catholic church – and since – everyone adopted a patron saint.
  Beatrice also hints that she will change her bridegroom.
beholding Beholden, obliged.
discourse Conversation.
deserved i.e. by pleasing Beatrice.
article between Condition to be settled.
Your country Where you come from.
strength Fortifications.

promonts' tops The tops of hills.

native Of the same country.

He was … truth Beatrice is Vermandero's 'best love' – so he speaks truer than he knows. A typical piece of word-play.

Iulan down A beard. The Greek word 'ioulos' means the first growth of beard.

silver i.e. grey hair.

went together Were alike.

Saint Jacques St James, patron saint of Spain.

I … him I was not as good.

Swallowed Killed.

Hollanders Holland, at one time a province of the Spanish Empire, fought long for freedom.

Whose i.e. his father's.

the late league The recent treaty of peace between Spain and the Dutch (1609).

breathe Relax (from fighting).

hot Eagerly.

violent Hasty.

toy A small matter. Vermandero's words become ironic: the matter of Beatrice's virginity turns out to be crucially important.

Not changed You haven't changed your mind.

entertainment Hospitality.

let's on Let's continue.

poisons A recurrent image. The poison at work in the play is lust. These lines echo I,1,114–5.

occasions Opportunities.

I shall be sorry Beatrice has a deeper meaning: she wants him at the wedding as bridegroom, not guest.

not so suddenly i.e. when she's had time to get rid of Alonzo.

ornaments Accomplishments.

Bound Obliged. In the next line Vermandero uses the word in its other sense: attached.

I'll … else Otherwise I'll not have my way.

murderers Small cannon – but Alsemero refers to Vermandero's words.

But … go This is a recognition of fate: Alsemero is so smitten he must submit.

a favour A token.

thrust … sockets There is an evident sexual innuendo here.

hates me … love her This opposition of love and hate is typical of the play's violent emotions. But their closeness is also hinted at, and the passage echoes lines 112–129.

I'll have my will Compare 225–226. 'Will' in the sense of 'desire' plays a major role in the play.

Act I Scene 2

Alibius, the owner of an asylum, explains to his assistant Lollio that he wants to keep his young wife Isabella away from inquisitive men. Lollio promises to help him, by watching her. They receive into the asylum a new inmate Antonio, a simpleton. The scene ends with the madmen calling for their dinner.

Commentary

If the first scene leads us to expect comedy, the second does so even more – and comedy of a rather low sort. Madness was a popular topic in 17th-century drama, for both comic and tragic writers. And the mismatch between an old husband and a young wife is a theme as old as comedy itself. Alibius is a classic old fool, treated as such by his assistant, who is himself rather dim – though sharper than his master. The asylum houses both madmen and fools (simpletons), and this offers plenty of opportunity for word-play, which is a feature of the comic scenes in *The Changeling*; they depend heavily on puns and misunderstandings.

Characterization is negligible; instead we are deliberately given caricatures, immediately recognizable to a contemporary audience. However, apart from their minor interest as comedy, these scenes serve another purpose. They form a kind of anti-masque or comic commentary on the main action. The play invites us to compare Beatrice and Isabella, Alibius and Alonzo, De Flores and Lollio etc.; and to think about adultery, betrayal, sexual attraction and love as both comic and tragic subjects. They also offer a balance to the elevated proceedings among the great with a 'slice of life' – albeit of a rather hackneyed kind.

close to Careful with.
nearer More intimate.
sweeter This is a kind of transferred epithet; Alibius is about to describe his wife as a temptation to men.
handle Discuss.
go about Intend to do.
So much ... secret Lollio means that pleasing a young wife is something for an old man to be proud of: his replies often hint at the bawdy.
meet'st Touch on.
No sir ... old Lollio This is typical of the farcical elements in the scene.
this i.e. the fact that Alibius is old and his wife young.

the old trees ... higher ... ring A bawdy pun. A young wife is more likely to betray an old husband, thus producing 'cuckold's horns' which would grow high. Alibius continues the pun: 'ring' refers both to the wedding-ring and to female genitalia.
thrusting Compare I,1,240 above.
conceiv'st Understand – but again, perhaps, a pun.
eye The many references to eyes and seeing are here linked to spying.
look out Two senses: (i) look out for his wife's misbehaviour; (ii) go outside the house on business. Lollio takes up the pun.
treadings Comings and goings.
Supply my place Lollio later tries to do this sexually. The phrase commonly occurs in this sense.
surely Certainly.
comfortable Comforting.
whip Whipping was a common 'cure' for madness, and a way of controlling simpletons.
fools and ... fools The word-play here is frequently echoed later. A knave is one who behaves badly, often lecherously. Lollio means that the fools aren't bright enough to misbehave and the madmen haven't enough sense to 'fool' with women.
care Worry.
thrift Prosperity.
visitants Visitors.
gallants Amorous young men.
habits Clothes.
shrewd Formidable.
answered Avoided.
ward Solution. That Alibius couldn't think of this himself suggests his own foolishness.
by that consequent As a result of that.
fool ... madman Lollio's reply hints that Alibius's wife knows what's what.
buckler Shield i.e. Lollio's solution to the problem.
pluck a rose Pass water.
Profoundly Well said.
scholars i.e. the inhabitants of the asylum.
entered i.e. on the role.
Save you Short for 'God save you'.
speaks Expresses.
takes off Relieves.
commodious Suitable.
sick ... nature i.e. his mind.
patterns Examples.
charge Cost.
officer Servant.
marry Short for 'By Mary'.
no beast It is supposed that only human beings can laugh.

wit Sense.
might he … crutches If he could only manage to approach sense.
his own His own property.
attendance Service.
sweet Clean.
discretion Here and above (line 114) this means both 'understanding' and 'prudence'.
there … want No expense need be spared.
magnifico Grandee.
wind Raise.
constable A figure especially noted for his stupidity.
headborough A kind of inferior constable.
able him Enable him (to become).
keeper i.e. Lollio.
Why … it Pedro speaks ironically, of course. Lollio and his master are themselves fools.
go to As you like. This is a general phrase which can mean more or less anything, according to context.
arrant Unmitigated.
passing Very.
if I had … too A typically idiotic wise-sounding remark: 'If I weren't a fool I'd be less foolish.'
your best cares Your best attention.
none Alibius plays on the other meaning of care: 'trouble'.
cousin Kinsman. Here it also signifies 'keeper'.
thou be'st You are.
I were best I had better.
form The madhouse is run as a kind of school.
true Genuine.
deuce Pair.
goes to Both (i) constitute and (ii) visit.
parlous Perilous i.e. brighter than he seems.
beadle Parish officer (with the power to dispense justice for small offences).
served Baffled.
push-pin A children's game.
we three Once again Lollio plays on the meanings of fool and knave. He calls Alibius a knave between two fools.
Put's … pillory Put his head in the pillory.
the bread's too little i.e. we are hungry.
crag Neck.
Bedlam The name of a famous mental hospital, which became the usual name of all such places. The lunatics all refer to food or feeding.
wire Whip.
her permasant My cheese (parmesan). Supposed to be Welsh dialect.
your charge Those in your charge. Then Alibius uses the same word (line 222) in the sense of 'instruction'.

Of which ... I am? Do you take *me* for a fool or a madman? Lollio
  patronizes his master.
pretty Fine – used ironically.
stultus The Latin for 'foolish' – Lollio declines the verb.

Revision questions on Act I

1 Briefly describe the relationships presented in Act I and say
how they are established.

2 How is the character of Beatrice presented in this Act?

3 Can you identify any recurring images in Act I, Scene 1? If
so, what are they, and what is the effect of their recurrence?

4 What use is made of social distinctions in this Act?

5 What relation does I,1 bear to I,2?

Act II Scene 1

Through Jasperino, Beatrice makes an arrangement to meet
his master. De Flores enters, meditating upon his ugliness, to
announce the arrival of Beatrice's betrothed, Alonzo de Piracquo. Once again she spurns the servant, and comments (aside)
on her irrational intense loathing for him. Vermandero brings
on Alonzo and his brother, Tomazo, and it is agreed that the
wedding will be postponed by three days. When the brothers
are left alone, Tomazo immediately expresses his doubts about
Beatrice, but his claim that she is indifferent to his brother is
angrily rejected by Alonzo, who swears vengeance against anyone who insults her.

Commentary

The conflict between De Flores and Beatrice is explored
further, and they are both given extended soliloquies, carefully
contrasted. Beatrice expatiates on the nature of 'true love'
while De Flores asserts that far uglier men than he are loved by
women, and remarks on his hard fate. Both speeches are filled
with visual imagery, which becomes ironic in the light of
exchanges between the Piracquo brothers: Alonzo literally cannot 'see' what Tomazo sees – that Beatrice hardly even looks at
him. Throughout the scene Beatrice's inability to control her

desires becomes more and more apparent – as does her effect on the desires of others.

severally Separately.
conduct Set of instructions.
return Produce.
bosom Metonym for 'person'.
discreet Prudent. The speech is thoroughly ironic. Alsemero's love proves to be far from prudent – and Beatrice herself turns out to be both reckless and misguided in her choice of De Flores as an accomplice.
the eyes of judgement See I,1,73 *et seq.*
In darkness ... love The worst thing for a lover is the beloved's absence, but you can tell true love from its power to evoke the beloved even when absent.
spends ... for Wastes his breath on.
his blessing ... name His blessing is only given to me insofar as I have regard for his reputation (by marrying where he chooses).
Some ... remembered I must think of a plan quickly.
forward Pressing.
that way i.e. Vermandero is hurrying his daughter into marriage with Piracquo.
my new comforts i.e. Alsemero.
force Think up.
into her sight Like Beatrice, De Flores is preoccupied with eye-imagery. She is beautiful, he is ugly.
At no hand In no way.
But I ... doted on But I know people with far worse faces who don't have to put up with them in loneliness, but are even doted on by others.
pick-haired Bristly.
swine Swinish. In this very muddled metaphor the deformity is compared to swine swilling in wrinkle-like troughs filled with water (wash) from dishonest eyes – implying that the eyes of De Flores are honest: ironic, under the circumstances.
And has ... sweet And is beautiful in the eyes of his sweetheart.
storm of hail i.e. Beatrice's hard looks and words.
Soft and fair De Flores is addressing Beatrice.
standing toad-pool An allusion to De Flores's face.
shower See above, line 55.
amain Violently.
another since Yet another.
Too soon De Flores means too soon for him.
Garden-bull Paris Garden, south London, was a great centre for bull- and bear-baiting. See line 32 above.
lugged Baited.
bad Ugly.

beyond all reason Ironically, all the passions in the play – both love and hatred – are beyond all reason.

chops Cheeks.

'mongst his fellows i.e. with Beatrice.

abed to Into bed with. De Flores' comment on the perversity of women is typical of 17th-century satire, but also appropriate to Beatrice's contrariness.

of … after For an hour after. It is typical of Beatrice to react in such an extreme, even pathological manner.

fiercer torrent i.e. her obligation to marry Piracquo instead of Alsemero.

improved Both (1) made good use of (by marrying Beatrice) and (2) made better (by being so worthy).

suddenly Both Vermandero and his daughter, for different reasons, harp on the rapid approach of the marriage.

keep Guard against.

night In apposition to Vermandero's 'day', Beatrice remains preoccupied with the wedding-night.

If it … near me She is already determined to avoid it.

troth Truth.

eye See.

bringing on you Convincing you.

ill-set Badly printed. Alonzo means that lovers should overlook small faults.

faults Misprints.

my son Vermandero rubs salt into his daughter's wound by already claiming Alonzo as a son.

motion Request.

maidenhead Virginity.

far out of reason Unreasonable. Presumably Vermandero thinks Beatrice wishes to get to know Alonzo a little better. She is playing for time.

former time is pinching The original date is a little hasty.

Though … forward Although my happiness has been postponed as many days as I'd prefer it brought forward.

as pleasing i.e. to Alonzo.

it i.e. Alonzo's 'gladness'.

in that point In that state.

So … parting More alert than his brother, Tomazo knows there is something wrong.

dullness Indifference.

exceptious Prone to take exception.

your harms Offences against you.

cozened Cheated, conned.

bring it to Bring to it.

half-father In the seventeenth century it was believed that children were affected by their parents' thoughts and passions at the moment of conception.

get 'em Beget them.

in his passions This seems to refer to 'her passions for him' – thus though the lover's passions cannot be literally realized in the act of conception, the woman's passions for him (*his* passions) do play a part in procreation.

how dangerous … time to How dangerous and shameful her behaviour will become in time if her true passions are restrained.

an If.

An enemy Alonzo is clearly another creature of strong passions: he refuses to see what is so clear to his brother.

w'are bound We are bound – because of the close blood-relationship.

madness Tomazo's allusion hints at a link with the asylum scenes, made explicit later.

vexation Torment.

Act II Scene 2

Beatrice meets Alsemero, who offers to challenge Alonzo. Beatrice rejects this plan as too dangerous, but then realizes that De Flores is the man to dispose of Alonzo. De Flores enters and she soon flatters him into eagerly offering to commit murder. She leaves and Alonzo enters. De Flores agrees to show him round the castle.

Commentary

This scene shows very clearly the contrast between Alsemero's honourable way of going about things, and Beatrice's instinctive turning to underhand methods. She is blind to any possible consequences, alive only to the fulfulment of her own desires. She takes no note of De Flores's surprising enthusiasm to serve a woman who has always disdained him. On the contrary, reckoning without De Flores's extreme recklessness – his passions are at least as strong as hers – she assumes it will be easy to get rid of him after the murder.

Th'are dangerous things It would be dangerous – because too much praise of Alsemero would make Beatrice jealous of Diaphanta: another hint at the violence of her passions.

These Such.

locked Compare II,1,11. This becomes ironic in retrospect when Diaphanta is betrayed by Beatrice because she knows too much.

within Before.

furnish our defects Remedy our wants.

W'are . . . expressions We are so similar in (1) what we have to say and (2) our means of saying it.

an enemy It is not clear whether Beatrice means her suitor or his brother. Either way, she exaggerates: neither of them knows about Alsemero. They are *potential* enemies.

go near i.e. go near to saying it.

the cause i.e. her betrothal to Piracquo.

find Understand.

piece 'bout Attribute of.

ventured At risk.

That's Who are.

you're danger's You are in danger – because he would have killed Piracquo.

obscurity Banishment.

keep Withhold.

condition Type.

a course i.e. what Alsemero proposed.

to bring . . . death To end my sorrow by killing me with grief.

ne'er ha'dried Never have dried.

dust i.e. of the grave.

a fouler visage An uglier appearance – a phrase which foreshadows the part played by De Flores.

And now . . . to blame Beatrice suddenly realizes that if she had been kinder to De Flores, he would be the man for the job.

ha'marred Have spoilt.

yet to see . . . be Yet I couldn't see as much as that.

of art Ingenious.

keep Use.

sure of our side Propitious for us.

the time opens An opportunity presents itself.

t'other Alonzo.

served Suited – but with a sexual undertone.

I'll put in for one I'll try for my chance (with Beatrice).

spreads and mounts Sexual innuendo is here mixed with the notion that a woman who copulates with more than one man will copulate with any number.

like arithmetic In arithmetical progression.

sutler Purveyor of provisions.

put case Put the case that.

him i.e. De Flores.

serve my turn upon Achieve my purpose through. But there is also an ironic hint of sexual innuendo. (See II,2,60)

a-late Recently.

Y'ave You have.

pruned Improved.

amorously Ironic: Beatrice means 'attractive' but De Flores does indeed look amorously on her.

physnomy Physiognomy i.e. face.

heat of the liver Beatrice refers to the growths on De Flores's face. But the liver is the seat of the passions: again she speaks more truly than she knows.

a water A lotion.

an act of pleasure A sexual act.

hard Plain.

mends Improves.

on't Of it.

If cause were of If it is caused by.

service The word has sexual overtones. Compare line 60 above, and note the use of 'mounts' in the next line.

mounts Amounts.

on't i.e. of the previous sigh.

too quick The banter in this passage has strong sexual overtones: Beatrice sighing coquettishly and De Flores becoming more insistent.

would fain Desires to.

lend it a free word Set it free with a word.

creation Beatrice becomes more provocative with each remark, and De Flores takes her up.

that's it He takes creation in the sense of 'procreation'.

not it Beatrice's wish is the last thing De Flores desires.

my loathings What produces loathings in me.

so much man Double entendre: De Flores would like to prove Beatrice a woman by demonstrating his virility. He also equates manhood with valour – compare I,2,27.

small cause It is difficult to tell whether this is ironic – Beatrice's distaste surfacing – or whether she is simply egging him on.

Put ... me Do not deprive me of it.

service ... kneel Again double entendre: (i) he literally kneels to beg her good will; (ii) he hints at the man kneeling between the woman's thighs in copulation.

blood and danger She speaks again truer than she knows.

sue Beg.

any act See II,2,88.

charge on't Responsibility of it.

Belike Perhaps.

wants are greedy Either (1) desires are large, or (2) needs are great.

his need Beatrice means his need for gold – but we know that his need for her is far stronger.

forward Eager.

Thy reward Again Beatrice means money and De Flores means sexual favours.

ravishes The word makes his expectations explicit.

lovely Ironic: Beatrice's lust for someone else makes an ugly murderer seem beautiful to her.

Dearlier Ironic: Beatrice is to pay a higher price than she dreams of.

upon the cast i.e. of the dice.
I throw Beatrice takes up his metaphor.
his dog-face i.e. De Flores's.
Slovenly Sloppy.
odd feeders De Flores notes Beatrice's perversity. Just as he 'thirsted'
  for Alonzo's death, so he thinks of Beatrice 'feeding' sexually. The
  image recurs.
supperless i.e. without sexual pleasure.
ha'met Have met.
strength Fortifications.
straits Narrow passages – this anticipates De Flores's plan to kill
  Alonzo.
Push An exclamation such as 'No' or 'Never' etc.
'gainst In anticipation of.
rising i.e. from dinner.
thrust upon In my clutches.

Revision questions on Act II

1 In what ways does the relationship between Beatrice and De
Flores change or develop in this Act?

2 Analyse De Flores's long speech at II,1,26–51, paying
particular attention to imagery and language. What do we learn
about De Flores from the speech?

3 Examine the role played by sexual imagery in this Act.

4 What relevance do Beatrice's lines at II,1,89–96 have for the
play as a whole and this Act in particular?

5 Describe the character of Alonzo and say what part he plays in
this Act.

Act III Scene 1

Alonzo and De Flores enter, at the beginning of their tour round
the castle. De Flores checks that he has all the keys and then
makes sure that both he and Alonzo hang up their swords. In
the meantime he hides a third sword, ready to commit murder.

Commentary

The murder of Alsemero is prepared in this scene, which is little
more than a prelude to what follows.

In the Act-time In the interval between two Acts.
wanted Been without (the key).
postern Back door.
sconce A small fortress.
You'll ... more i.e. when we're past this bit. But the remark is ironic:
  Alonzo will soon be dead.

Act III Scene 2

They continue their tour and De Flores takes the opportunity to
stab Alonzo. He tries to take a diamond ring off the corpse:
when it won't budge he cuts off the whole finger, then leaves
with the body.

Commentary

The scene makes clear De Flores's complete ruthlessness. Not
only has he no qualms about the murder: he calmly mutilates the
body to get at the ring, then drags the body out of the room. In
these two short scenes (III,1; III,2) the central deed of the play
is performed. What we see afterwards is the working out of
consequences, as they enmesh Beatrice and De Flores and draw
them together.

A place ... on De Flores's grim humour.
house Household.
makes up Constitutes.
bastard i.e. inferior.
you may dwell The immediate meaning is 'you may look' but the
  grimmer sense is 'you may stay'.
I am upon't I can see it. In the next line De Flores takes these words in
  another sense: 'I am doing it.'
silence This becomes ironic later in the play when the ghost of Alonzo
  appears: he is 'silenced' but not obliterated.
a diamond See II,1,15.
approve the work Prove the job done.
suspect or fear Evidence (which would make me fear causing
  suspicion).

Act III Scene 3

Lollio tells Isabella that Alibius has instructed him to keep her at
home. She therefore demands that Lollio shall at least amuse
her by parading some of the asylum inmates. He introduces

Franciscus, a mad poet, who praises Isabella extravagantly with crazy parodies of conventional poetic language. When Isabella tires of him, Lollio takes him out and brings in Antonio. When Lollio goes out to attend to the lunatics, Antonio reveals that he is really sane and has assumed a disguise so as to reach Isabella. Lollio returns and questions the 'fool' Antonio for Isabella's entertainment. When he goes out again, Antonio renews his suit to Isabella, but Lollio returns unperceived and observes them kissing. He leaves, and the madmen briefly enter disguised as birds and beasts. Lollio takes Antonio away, then comes back and tries Isabella himself, quoting Antonio's words to show he has overheard them. She rejects him. Alibius then enters, announcing that he has been commissioned to provide an entertainment for Beatrice's wedding, using the fools and madmen.

Commentary

The parodic function of the sub-plot is developed further. Sexual desire, which motivates the tragedy, is here treated comically, and we are invited by the juxtaposition to compare the two treatments. Once again we have an attractive woman (Isabella), a deceived partner (Alibius), suitors (Antonio and Franciscus), and a servant (Lollio) on the look-out for his own reward. The scene makes use of various comic strategies: fake madness, the parade of disguised madmen, Lollio's eavesdropping, and the parallel attempts of Antonio, Franciscus and Lollio to make love to Isabella. She is the one character developed in a little depth in these comic scenes, showing wit and resourcefulness.

sirrah A contemptuous form of 'sir'.
commission Authority.
pipe after Follow my lead.
pinfold Enclosure (for cattle).
pounded Impound — but with the cheeky subordinate sense of 'seduced'. Lollio takes up Isabella's sarcastic animal metaphor.
very wise This is ironic.
a madman . . . fool Isabella revives the wearisome humour of I,2.
participate of Be partly. Lollio hints that he is the danger to Alibius's honour.
mad . . . foolish Lollio uses the words in the senses of 'reckless' and 'misbehaved'.
brave Daring.
Afford Show.

proper Handsome.

your wisdom Again, this is ironic.

a match The same as.

o'the'side In addition.

shooting a bolt An allusion to the saying, 'A fool's bolt is soon shot.'

wrinkle Furrow.

Anacreon ... spider The classical Greek poet Anacreon was supposed to have choked on a grape-stone while drinking wine. Spiders were all thought to be poisonous.

pretty Fine.

set him forwards Advanced him.

neither Anyway.

Titania The queen of the fairies.

Oberon Titania's husband.

Dryades Wood nymphs. This speech is a parody of 17th-century pastoral verse.

Diomed A Thracian king who fed his horses with human flesh.

Bucephalus The famous charger of Alexander the Great. Franciscus makes his speeches from a tissue of conventional classical references, appropriate to a mad poet.

Esculapius Greek god of healing and medicine.

poison i.e. the whip.

Tiresias A Theban soothsayer who changed into a woman and back again. Juno, queen of the gods, is supposed to have blinded him for saying women took more pleasure than men in sexual intercourse. The suitability of this reference to the play is evident.

might Might be.

an eye i.e. she can see more.

Luna The moon-goddess.

two trades Madness and blindness.

big-bellied Pregnant, i.e. the moon is full.

Hecate Evil aspect of the moon-goddess.

Dog ... bush The dog and bush belonged to the man in the moon.

lycanthropi Werewolves.

while Both (1) way, and (2) period of time.

aunt Slang for 'whore'.

uncle Slang for 'pander'.

nigget Idiot.

bauble Stick (phallic in shape).

Ever since ... cousin Antonio speaks the exact truth.

left-handed Orlando Orlando is the mad hero of Ariosto's poem *Orlando Furioso* (1516). Since left-handed can also mean 'awkward', the phrase seems to signify that Lollio will pretend to be one of the madmen, i.e. that he will lay about him, to reduce them to order.

Amazing Amazed.

shape of folly Pretence of madness.

your dearest love The one who loves you most dearly.

a fine fool Isabella means that (1) he is no fool and (2) he really *is* a fool for behaving like this.

scrutinous Investigative.

like/A cunning poet Antonio here states the Renaissance idea of the poet (found in Sidney and elsewhere) as one who combines all other branches of knowledge into the supreme art of poetry.

parlous Extreme.

stand you Allow you.

fashioned out Devised.

And this i.e. pretending to be a fool to gain admittance to the asylum.

Galaxia Galaxy.

withal As well.

you dreamed Isabella remains ironic.

acquaintance Notice.

habit Both 'dress' and 'manner'.

As Insofar as.

valentine Suitor. Antonio is now speaking in his character as a fool.

Passing Very.

hold on Continue – Isabella refers to his wooing as well as his madness.

put him to't Put him to the test.

couple in hell Allusion to a popular game of 'catch as catch-can'.

posture Manner, i.e. as a fool.

you become … clothes Speaking seriously does not suit you.

from i.e. out of character with.

Lives (Who) lives.

Hesperides Mythological guardians of golden apples, sought by Hercules as one of his twelve labours.

giants The giant Atlas was father of the Hesperides.

Lipsius Famour scholar – but Lollio is making a joke about lips.

Ars Amandi *The Art of Love*, a long poem in three books, by Ovid.

Do you Imperative.

wanton Flirt.

dress … up See myself. By looking into her eyes he will see his true self, not dressed as an idiot.

bright mirrors i.e. her eyes.

array me Dress myself.

Cuckoo This is an aside, indicating that Lollio thinks his master is about to be cuckolded.

Madmen above Now follows a scene characteristic of 17th-century tragedy – a tableau of madmen.

Of fear Frightening.

conceit Fancy.

no fears Not frightening.

a large one A 'fear', i.e. Lollio.

benefices Church-livings.

put you down Double entrendre: (1) answer back, (2) make love to.

current i.e. the current of her desires.

bankers Labourers who build river banks.
stray i.e. from the path of virtue.
needle's point i.e. of the compass. There is a double entendre here, the 'needle' being also the penis.
arctics The magnetic poles.
sweet rogue Lollio, like De Flores, decides to try his own luck.
have at thee Let me try!
follow now Follow his words, i.e. speak. Lollio quotes Antonio's words.
Lacedemonian One who speaks succinctly.
a thing i.e. female genitalia.
knight-errant i.e. Antonio.
adventure Advance.
purchase Winning.
For me enjoying If he wishes to enjoy me. Compare Beatrice's use of De Flores.
do it Submit to his embraces.
fool's part Double entendre: (1) share (2) sexual intercourse. The 'fool's part' is the penis. See line 242 above.
bounden Bonded, i.e. slave.
nearly Closely.
bespoke our pains Commanded our labours.
fag Conclusion.
unexpected ... over i.e. the entrance of the madmen will be a surprise.
frightful pleasure Oxymoron: frightening pleasure.
act ... teach it i.e. the performance.
measure Dance.
breaking time's head i.e. being out of time (personification).
This This will be the result.
begun Offered to begin with.
And will ... known And if we put on a good performance we will earn even more.
their wits ... heads They are brighter with their feet than with their brains.
Y'ave ... on't You have a good business there. Again Isabella speaks contemptuously.

Act III Scene 4

Vermandero anounces his affection for Alsemero, which is noted by Beatrice. De Flores then enters and tells her that Alonzo is disposed of. He shows her the diamond ring, still on Alonzo's severed finger, and she tells him to keep the jewel, promising him further reward. De Flores is furious: it is not monetary reward he wants, but Beatrice herself. She resists his demands, offering him all her wordly wealth if he will leave her alone. But De Flores points out that they are now associates in crime, and that he will betray her if she does not oblige him. The scene ends with Beatrice's tacit acceptance that this is the case.

Commentary

As Beatrice justly remarks, this is the scene in which 'Vengeance begins'. She starts to reap the consequences of her thoughtless lust. Yet it is also the scene in which she advances Alsemero in her father's affections. Thus in one scene Beatrice moves from the apparently upward to the clearly downward slope. This encapsulates the play's tragic irony: that it is precisely in encompassing her desire that Beatrice works her own downfall. De Flores, in contrast, here takes his chance with both hands: yet for him, too, this is the beginning of the end. Ironically De Flores, a far more clear-sighted and realistic person than Beatrice, does not see this. It is worth comparing this scene with *Othello* III,3, in which Iago gradually persuades Othello to agree to his schemes. There, too, we find a remarkably vivid and subtle picture of a relationship's psychology: Iago, like De Flores, gradually imposes his will on his social superior.

I wish ... for you Vermandero's words are an example of dramatic irony.
creature Not impolite in 17th-century usage.
her fellow Unclear whether he means his wife or another daughter.
vale Vale of sin, i.e. the world.
my ... in In which I take most pleasure.
largely Everywhere.
one step i.e. his kind greeting of Alsemero.
fix him i.e. fix Alsemero in her father's favour.
wisdom ... freedom In view of coming events, another instance of dramatic irony.
eye be darkened A euphemism for 'when Alonzo is dead'.
refulgent virtue Radiant influence, Beatrice is fooling herself. She uses the word virtue to mean 'benevolent force' but imperceptibly surrenders to its ethical implications – which we, the audience, know to be false. It is appropriate that as she speaks De Flores should enter with his news.
at a banquet i.e. feasting on the reward in prospect.
For ... for't Compared with the reward I promise myself for it.
answerable Suitable.
at mine eyes Beatrice weeps with pleasure – and perhaps from stress. But she is *looking* at De Flores – so her remark is ironic: this is where her *trouble* begins.

born weeping Like children.
'Tis soon applied i.e. the principle of rewarding the 'keeper'.
capcase A small travelling case.
from the worm i.e. the worm of guilt.
the way on't Such a thing.
In state of By way of.
to't For it.
strange De Flores is ironic.
cause i.e. of comment.
one of my performance Someone who has done what I have.
warm This could be either 'eager' or 'recent' – or both. In any case,
  De Flores is ironic.
you cause With the 'you' emphasized – she means 'cause to be
  offended'.
sharp Aggravated.
meanly thought upon Both 'underestimated' and 'despised'.
salary Payment. De Flores is furious that Beatrice should think to
  reward him with anything less than herself.
How What do you mean?
journeyman Day labourer.
brought home i.e. done by someone else.
than I was i.e. before she persuaded him to do the murder.
my fear i.e. of detection.
thou be'st You are.
in … as I I'm sure you are as deep in guilt as I am.
were Would be.
home The truth.
so jointly De Flores is bullying Beatrice. He has no way of proving that
  she suborned him, and the ring alone would suggest theft as a motive
  if he fled, without implicating her. This is weak plotting. On the other
  hand, the strength of De Flores's character, his intensity, and her
  fright at what has been done, may all combine to unbalance her
  judgement.
strange Distant, reserved.
This i.e. her coldness.
doubt Fear.
stand Wait.
forgetfulness i.e. of where and who they are.
betray us Beatrice implicitly accepts their joint responsibility.
forgetful He means that she forgets her responsibility to him.
eased Relieved. In line 100 he uses the word in another sense: 'be
  eased of' means 'take sexual pleasure with'.
in pain With unsatisfied desire.
Justice Ironic under the circumstances. De Flores means reward.
lose Not hear. Beatrice reveals a characteristic ability for self-
  deception.
The last i.e. the previous murder (of Alonzo).

into spirit In spirits.
wrought Worked.
why . . . took Why did I bother to take so much trouble?
piteously Very much indeed.
In order In due course.
after . . . of Behind.
resolved Certain.
his death i.e. Alonzo's. De Flores is claiming the love of Beatrice as his reward – the more embarrassing for her as she is about to be married. In theory the seventeenth century set a very high price on female virginity.
A woman . . . modesty? This brutal reply cuts through all her evasions of the truth. It also expresses the play's equation of sex with violence.
living Beatrice makes the point: she *is* bound to Alonzo because he is dead.
the distance i.e. the distance in breeding. But earlier in the play De Flores claims to be a gentleman by birth (II,1,49).
equal De Flores here makes a crucial point: separated by birth, he and Beatrice are on the same *moral* level. By wishing the death of Alonzo she has put herself in the servant's power.
to me In favour of me.
the deed's creature This superb phrase expresses Beatrice's predicament exactly.
by the name In that role.
first condition Innocence. De Flores intimates that moral innocence and sexual purity go together: Beatrice has forfeited both.
I challenge you i.e. to admit the truth of what he is saying.
peace . . . turned you out Cast you off. De Flores makes Beatrice not the former possessor of these qualities but their object. This is in line with the 'deed's creature' spirit of his words: that she is now a kind of thing, a moral victim.
one with Both 'the same as' and 'joined to'.
fair murd'ress This is oxymoron.
urge Provoke.
writ'st Call yourself.
he's changed i.e. Alonzo – from life to death.
Whom . . . enjoy'st You will never take your pleasure with him unless I take mine with you.
darkness Wickedness.
my life . . . nothing This is the danger Beatrice has not reckoned with: that De Flores is as passionate as she, and a good deal more reckless. He has nothing to lose but an unpleasant life.
shooting eye Once again eye-imagery is made explicit: De Flores cannot resist the fire burning in his mistress's eyes.
She . . . be Note the rhyming couplet which gives emphasis to this solemn warning.
honour i.e. chaste.

weep fate Move fate by your tears.

Vengeance Beatrice's words accurately mark the next stage of this revenge tragedy. But they are truer than she knows, for the vengeance will also be worked on De Flores himself.

engender Copulate.

a viper i.e. De Flores.

shroud The verb is appropriate: Beatrice must 'kill' her shame.

best receipts Best recipes.

Thy peace ... yielding The play will reveal the irony of this remark.

turtle Turtle-dove – always a symbol of love. De Flores refers to Beatrice's sobbing – with a certain degree of irony.

Thou'lt ... on The last couplet brings together love and hate.

Revision questions on Act III

1 Describe exactly what happens in III,4 and give the reasons for it.

2 What is important about the scenes in the madhouse in Act III, and what relation do they have to the other parts of the Act?

3 Compare the roles of Beatrice and Isabella in this Act.

4 Give any four examples of striking imagery or language used in this Act and say what is important or unusual about them.

5 How far can we sympathize with Beatrice in this Act?

Act IV Scene 1

The disappearance of Alonzo Piracquo, the marriage of Beatrice and Alsemero, and the appearance of Alonzo's ghost to De Flores, to whom he shows his mutilated hand, are all enacted in dumb-show. Beatrice then enters, meditating on what will happen when Alsemero discovers on their wedding-night that she is not a virgin. It becomes clear that she has allowed De Flores to make love to her. She comes to Alsemero's private room, unlocks the door and goes in. There she finds a potion that is said to reveal whether or not girls who take it are virgins. She tries it on herself and on her maid, Diaphanta, who claims to be intact. Sure enough, Diaphanta shows the symptoms predicted for virgins: Beatrice, who also takes the potion, does not. In the meantime, Beatrice also proposes that Diaphanta should take her place in the nuptial bed, in return for reward. The maid, eager for both money and sexual pleasure, agrees.

Commentary

Antonius Mizaldus was a real person, who did indeed write the book quoted in this scene – which is a good example of the use that 17th-century dramatists made of contemporary material. On the other hand, this kind of plot device really seems to belong in the comic part of the play. Effectively, all the action, save for the dénouement, is over: to fill their five acts the writers stretch their material a little. However, the potion is a vivid way of dramatizing Beatrice's plight and the increasingly complex schemes she is forced to pursue in order to disguise it. We are invited to compare her anguish with Diaphanta's simple lust: from the same motive, but by different routes, the two eventually meet the same fate. Diaphanta is another of the play's changelings, substituting for Beatrice in the marriage bed. The contrast of the stately beautiful Beatrice with the lively straightforward Diaphanta is pointed: Beatrice has lost the impetus of her original desire in a web of intrigue.

(DUMB SHOW) A common element in Jacobean drama. It adds variety, gets through a good deal of action economically, and contributes to the ritualistic quality of the play.
after all Following behind.
accident Incident.
in the midst ... smile Thus is the power of conscience starkly dramatized. The notion that the ghosts of the murdered will not sleep until avenged is frequently the basis of the dénouement in Revenge plays – most famously in *Hamlet*.
endlessly Both 'for good' and 'incessantly'.
th'ensuing The following, i.e. her wedding night.
cope with Encounter.
plague Trouble. See III,4,152.
fault i.e. her lost virginity.
dive/into Dwell upon.
what course soe'er Whatever course of action.
Without ... danger Which will not make my shame (lost virginity) a cause of great danger.
use Treat.
precious Worthless (ironic).
die Dice.
gamester Gambler.
in't i.e. in the lock.
right Real.
vials Small glass bottles.
her mark Marked.

physic Medicine.

so 'tis, 'tis so Untranslatable, but meaning something like 'It is, too'.

the place suspicious i.e. because Alsemero has obviously been thinking about this problem.

beguile Puzzle.

look to Take note of.

Belike Probably.

Antonius Mizaldus The French author of *Secrets in Nature* (1520–78).

incontinently gape Yawn irresistibly.

Where had I been What would have happened if this had been tried on me?

it Unclear whether Beatrice fears such a test or her first night with Alonzo.

Cuds Corruption of 'God's'.

nice piece Scrupulous girl.

look Look for.

such a cause i.e. imminent marriage.

compass Cover (in his walk).

roosting time Bedtime.

little lodge Bawdy innuendo: female genitalia.

pit-hole Grave. But see line 62 above.

thoughts Diaphanta means 'desires'.

fashion Way of behaving.

set light by Speak indifferently of.

ow'd 'em not Didn't own them.

You ... behind You ignore a matter (loss of virginity) that causes blushes when thought of.

beshrew Curse.

Do you ... sooth Do you really mean it?

Man ... unknown I'd never have married.

try ... were Test the cause of my fear, i.e. go in my place.

get's from't Has done it.

fly from't i.e. from the test.

lies A pun: (1) stands in for, (2) lies, (3) lies down.

humour Fancy.

by-bet ... in Side-bet to protect.

abroad Elsewhere.

honesty Chastity.

to me i.e. as your substitute.

stray Look.

too quick Sharp – in the sense of flirtatious.

urge Insult.

Bad enough then i.e. if Diaphanta is no more a virgin than her mistress, she's no virgin at all.

lightsome joys Giddy pleasures.

It stirs ... it It doesn't affect me at all, and I am most vulnerable to it (if Alsemero chooses to use the test).

Just Exactly.
circumscrib'd Pre-arranged.
accident Incident.
sit by't Go on with it.
It lays itself It works.
carriage Organization.
the burthen i.e. sexual intercourse.
use Take, i.e. in Alonzo's bed.
cool Recovered from the pleasure ('heat') of intercourse.
I'm for … fools Now I have a dowry I want a big (important) fool for a husband, not an insignificant one. The equating of all husbands with fools is characteristic of the period's presentation of lecherous women. Diaphanta's humorous approach is contrasted with Beatrice's seriousness.

Act IV Scene 2

Tomazo claims that his brother has been murdered in Vermandero's castle. The body has not been found, and Vermandero makes the counter-charge that Alonzo has humiliated Beatrice and her family by not turning up to the wedding. Vermandero then leaves, and Tomazo greets De Flores warmly, enquiring about Beatrice. De Flores leaves and Alsemero enters, to be challenged by Tomazo. After Tomazo's departure, Alsemero is told by his servant Jasperino about a loving conversation between De Flores and Beatrice overheard by him and his girlfriend Diaphanta. Alsemero cannot believe it, especially when he is overcome by the sight of Beatrice's beauty – but he resolves to test her with the potion that Beatrice discovered in the previous scene. She pretends to know nothing about the test, and fakes all the symptoms of virginity. Alsemero is satisfied of her innocence.

Commentary

At the core of this scene are two deceptions: Tomazo's and Alsemero's. It is ironic that Tomazo smiles on De Flores but challenges Alsemero, and this emphasizes the irrational nature of his responses – a point which is taken up later in the play, when he reacts violently against De Flores for no particular reason. De Flores puts this down to instinct. Tomazo's mistrust of Alsemero parallels Alsemero's mistrust of Jasperino, just as Tomazo's trust in De Flores matches Alsemero's in Beatrice.

These relationships continue in parallel until, later in the play, Alsemero reveals the identity of the killers to Tomazo. Such symmetry is typical of the play, and it stresses the essentially psychological and emotional nature of the drama. Notice, for example, that the main action – De Flores's love-making with Beatrice – is not shown: it is Alsemero's response we concentrate on. The only *event* of much significance is the curious testing of Beatrice's virginity – and in this case, too, it is only the *effects* of the potion we see – which leads to another of the play's confusions between appearance and reality.

cause i.e. for suspicion of his honour. The present cause is Alonzo's disappearance.

intending to Planning to go to.

The time accuses They left about the time of the murder.

faithfully In good faith (for).

apprehension Arrest.

suddenly At once.

stain Of guilt.

discover Reveal.

wingéd Speedy.

set on Harrassed.

hot Violent.

dearest bloods Closest relations, i.e. Alsemero and Beatrice.

snatched Quick – especially when compared with the delay Beatrice asked for previously, when betrothed to Alonzo.

indeed Vermandero reverses Tomazo's charge, implying that Alonzo has abandoned his daughter.

abuséd Deceived.

prepared Prepared for the wedding.

he left i.e. by his departure.

belief hurt 'em Trust was betrayed.

public Because it became apparent on the wedding-day.

fair Good.

alliance Family relationship.

The best The best thing about Vermandero's reply.

meet Base.

Honest The audience will recognize the dramatic irony in this. Compare Othello's naming of Iago in *Othello*.

kind and true See line 37 above.

purely i.e. he felt only love for me. De Flores compounds the irony.

a-killing on In the process of killing.

He ... me He reminds me of the murder so vividly.

jealousy Suspicion.

myself De Flores clearly takes a pleasure in this talk.

easy Easy-going.

round-packed Plump.
sinner … are De Flores affects the attitude of the tolerant male to fragile womanhood.
at no hand In no way.
ev'n o'erlays Even (his company) disturbs.
honest See line 37 above.
He'll … time i.e. he'll reveal Beatrice's guilt – which turns out to be the case.
glorious This is said ironically.
reckon Come to a reckoning.
cause i.e. for finding the way there.
liquor i.e. blood.
'lay Allay.
fiery thirst Compare II,2,136.
Appear … strangers I cannot understand.
business Cause.
his right i.e. marriage to Beatrice.
look Expect.
it His sword.
relieves me From worry about the omen.
keep/Mine i.e. to myself.
And … this And do without it in this matter. Then why did Jasperino mention it?
puts me on Makes me more impatient.
pretend Offer.
lending Paying.
out Off course.
prevent Anticipate (and therefore contradict).
challenge Stir up.
dangerous See II,1,146.
eyes … shoot See III,4,153.
touched Corrupt.
here i.e. in my bed.
to … hereof To make certain of the truth.
Chaldean Generic name for a soothsayer.
hang together Fit.
woman Maid (Diaphanta).
Delivered Described her.
weep out Tearfully make.
she i.e. Beatrice.
obscurely In the dark.
sweet voyage Wedding night.
Push … though Beatrice's appearance convinces Alsemero of her innocence – but a doubt lingers.
She's abused This moment is testimony to Beatrice's beauty, which so affects all the men in the play.
composition Mixture.

I'm ... cunning Now my ingenuity is tested.
virtue Power.
Treble qualitied Extremely powerful in all three stages.
virtuous Both 'powerful' and 'chaste'. Ironic.
takes Works.
melancholy i.e. the third stage of the potion's effects.
Keep Make a note of.
morning's womb Dawn.

Act IV Scene 3

Isabella shows Lollio her letter from Franciscus, in which he explains that he has only pretended to be mad, and that he loves her. Isabella and Lollio plan to frighten off both Franciscus and Antonio by dressing up Isabella as a lunatic. Lollio gives her the key of his wardrobe and she goes out. Alibius arrives to discuss the arrangements for Beatrice's wedding. When he leaves Antonio comes in, shortly followed by Isabella, dressed as a madwoman. She attacks Antonio, who repulses her. She then reveals herself, and repulses him. Isabella leaves and Antonio curses his mistake. Lollio promises to help, suggesting that if Antonio should frighten off Franciscus, Isabella will be grateful enough to grant him her favours. Antonio leaves and Franciscus enters. Lollio reads from his letter to Isabella, proving that Franciscus's passions are known; but he also agrees to help, suggesting that Isabella will favour Franciscus if he frightens away Antonio. Alibius returns to complete the wedding arrangements.

Commentary

The testing of Antonio and Franciscus in this scene parallels the testing of Beatrice in the last: Isabella's disguise is equivalent to Alsemero's potion. However, it has a different result, for it produces not a deception but the truth. Lollio then engages in further deceptions, which can be compared with Beatrice's substitution of Diaphanta in her wedding-night bed. The difference lies in the degree of violence: Beatrice's intrigues cost lives; Isabella's merely involve self-respect. The parallel roles of Lollio and De Flores are also in evidence: both act as 'fixers' for their mistresses.

the waiting moon The moon was supposed to affect madmen (hence 'lunatics'). Isabella holds a letter from Franciscus. Thus she means 'Is this letter the result of the moon, which watches (waits) over us?'

his inside…out What he says (in the letter) with (1) his appearance (2) the address on the letter.

The out's The outside of the letter.

To the bright…post As Lollio says, this is indeed 'madness' – of a poetic sort.

Andromeda She was rescued by Perseus from a dragon.

Knight of the Sun Hero of a popular Jacobean romance.

Scorpio The sign of the Zodiac controlling the sexual parts.

Aeolus God of the winds.

mark Note.

imperfect Because he is subject to a passion – love.

sun…grow As the sun makes plants grow, so her beauty causes his erection. The bawdy meaning causes Lollio's interjection.

transshapes Transforms.

in winter…ornaments Because he is pretending to be someone else.

spring Both 'come to life' and 'rise'.

bounties Kindness, generosity.

my cure i.e. through love.

or…himself i.e. if she doesn't respond.

little pains i.e. great pleasure.

privy to In the secret of.

minister Give treatment, by making love with Francisicus.

my thirds 'Thirds' meaning that 'first' and 'second' are taken by Alibius and her lover.

fall…fall Isabella means 'fall from grace' and Lollio puns with 'fall on top of you' (make love).

stand to my venture Both (1) stand by my attempt (2) sustain my erection.

deal…deal Again a pun. Isabella means 'handle' whereas Lollio means 'have intercourse with'.

the fair understanding Understand me properly.

use 'em Treat them. Lollio again puns in the next line with 'Abuse 'em!'

kindly Fairly.

fit…you Arrange yourself for them and I'll organize them for you.

Take…outside Treat me according to the way I'm dressed. (She is about to disguise herself.)

I'll…inside I'll leave the real you inside the disguise.

perfect Completely ready.

as…up In order to conclude.

miss Make a mistake.

The more…it The more ridiculous it is, the more people will like it, i.e. mistakes will only enhance the effect.

nice Proper.

pizzles Whips made from the bull's penis – with the obvious bawdy innuendo.

morris Morris dance.

their fooling There is, of course, a nice irony in teaching 'fools' to behave foolishly.

measure Dance.
brook Tolerate.
takes some pleasure Ambiguous, with a bawdy innuendo.
length ... short Liberty ... confined. But also a bawdy double
  entendre.
nose ... elephant Presumably this is a version of the cuckold's horns
  joke: Lollio makes naughty hints about what might happen if Alibius
  allows his wife more liberty.
footmanship Dance steps.
ride With the connotation 'have intercourse'.
Vault in Jump to.
honour Bow – as at the end of a dance.
hams Thighs.
Marry By Mary.
stiffened Developed. Squires and yeomen were the lowest orders of
  nobility.
caper Upward leap. Lollio then puns on the meaning of honour.
figure (1) Dance step; (2) face.
Hey Isabella is feigning madness. Most of what she says is nonsense.
he treads Antonio (dancing).
shough Shoo.
Icarus The son of Daedalus who flew too near the sun on wings his
  father had made. The wax melted and Icarus fell to earth. Isabella
  pretends Antonio is Icarus.
clue A reference to the thread Ariadne left to help Theseus out of the
  Cretan Labyrinth. Isabella jumbles up classical allusions.
coz Short for 'cousin'.
Poz Plague.
Endymion Beautiful youth with whom the moon-goddess fell in love.
unshapen Shapeless.
antic Clown.
frantic Madman.
as ... fury i.e. as full of passion as my assumed behaviour is full of
  madness.
beguile Deceive.
caparisons Clothing.
feigner Deceiver.
usher Keeper.
another while A while longer.
So I am Antonio feels he really is 'mad' now he has been rejected.
forbear Spare.
foxskin An allusion to the fox's wiliness.
arrant Extreme, i.e. Franciscus, who is as sane as Antonio.
earn Deserve.
ride A crude form of 'make love to'.
eased Rid.
I ... on't I shall make a good job of it.

station Manner, i.e. of madness.
Latona The mother of Diana, the moon-goddess. Here her name is substituted for Diana's.
counterfeit Faker.
discover Uncover, reveal.
mend Get better – said ironically.
destiny Lollio takes Franciscus's 'read' to mean interpret, as in 'reading palms'.
of counsel with In the confidence of.
yours Again Lollio takes Franciscus's word – 'hand' – in the sense of 'handwriting'.
pick Pick pockets.
give you over Give you up. Lollio means that he will no longer supervise Franciscus.
cast your water Analyse urine, like a doctor.
There ... wishes That is what I wish to provide.
meet Fight – again a pun.
well-favouredly Soundly.
reserve him Refrain from (beating) him.
He ... Hey Franciscus reverts to his feigned madness.
Well said Well done.
in a readiness Is everything ready?
one ... begged To 'beg a fool' was to request guardianship over him – which brought with it control of his estate. Alibius's 'friends' are powerful people who might put such business in his way.
fit Suit, i.e. the dancing to the music.

Revisions questions on Act IV

1 Explain the roles of the following characters in this Act: Diaphanta, Jasperino, Tomazo, Vermandero.

2 Why is there a dumb-show and what effect does it have?

3 Discuss the scenes using the virgin-testing potion, bearing in mind the critical view that these distract from the seriousness of the main action. Say whether you agree with this, giving your reasons.

4 Discuss the role of comedy in this Act.

5 What kinds of literary parody do we find in Act IV?

Act V Scene 1

Beatrice waits for her maid Diaphanta to return from Alsemero's bed on the wedding-night, so that Beatrice can creep in to take her place; but as the clock strikes one, two, and then three, Diaphanta still does not arrive. De Flores appears and makes a plan with Beatrice: they will rouse the house when he has set fire to Diaphanta's room. When the maid rushes back to her chamber, De Flores will take advantage of the confusion to kill her, covering the gun-shots with the excuse that he is clearing the burning chimney of soot by firing up it. They carry this plan through successfully, and De Flores makes sure that Diaphanta's body is burnt, so that she will seem to have died in the fire. Beatrice remarks that the maid was careless, and Vermandero and Alsemero suspect nothing, but promise De Flores a reward. Beatrice joins in their promise, thus distancing herself from De Flores.

Commentary

This is the most atmospheric scene of the play, and – as so often with Jacobean tragedy – set at night. Beatrice's first speech makes effective use of the chiming clock – ironically, speeding up time in order to make it seem to pass more slowly. It is in this scene that De Flores rises to his greatest heights of daring and enterprise and finally wins Beatrice's unstinting admiration, and even love: he emerges as a thoroughly dynamic character compared to the other men in the play – just as Lollio shows greater sense and initiative than the other men in Alibius's house. But both De Flores and Beatrice also reveal here their complete and selfish ruthlessness: they are prepared to throw away Diaphanta's life without further consideration if that will serve their cause. The scene is full of activity, which helps to dispel a little of the extreme tension of the opening – but only so that it can be wound up again at the play's end.

One i.e. 1 a.m.
by't i.e. in Alsemero's bed.
Makes ... right i.e. Diaphanta makes trouble by exploiting Beatrice's right to her husband.
pays Will pay.
No (There can be) no.
rule her blood Control her desires.
faith Loyalty. An ironic complaint under the circumstance.
two The night scene with striking clocks is highly dramatic and serves to raise the tension.
stave'em off Keep them away from.

game royal i.e. what is reserved for their betters.
harsh and hardy Proud and wilful.
fall'n off Given up.
not yet i.e. has she still not finished?
fares Makes love.
undone Ruined.
Phosphorus The morning star.
fall . . . ruin Invent some disaster (to distract attention).
There . . . else Otherwise our secret will be out.
force a rising Rouse the entire house.
there's no remedy There's no other solution.
Take . . . that What do you say to that?
give over all Give up the whole thing.
reach Plan.
fame's on fire Reputation is at stake.
rich Complete.
strikes . . . sure Makes everything certain.
light parcels Burning pieces of tarred canvas.
which . . . suspicious i.e. the fact she's away from her room.
piece high-charged Loaded fowling-piece.
cleanse i.e. by blowing the burning soot away.
'tis proper It would be appropriate (as a safety measure).
mark Target.
I'm forced . . . now The more violent and brutal De Flores becomes, the more Beatrice warms to him: he embodies the ugliness and violence of her own desires.
'Slid Short for 'God's blood'.
continuance i.e. in life. It therefore means 'safety'.
How for What about?
The deed . . . time This is a phrase like 'The hour will provide the man.' The time will provide opportunity.
purifies Refines. The *idea* of fire sharpens his invention. De Flores is enjoying the adventure: it stimulates him.
Watch . . . minute Watch for your opportunity.
mist A cloudy – or clouded – vision.
he i.e. De Flores.
Saint Sebastian's The church where the clock-tower is.
rare Admirable.
care Both 'consideration' and 'carefulness'.
east i.e. the sunrise.
my charge My ammunition.
Here's . . . loving Beatrice has moved on again from Alsemero.
well Happy.
reward This is ironic.
sweetness/The fire The juxtaposition of these two ideas – sweetness and fire – is suggestive of pleasure and passion, accompanied by danger.

tremble Beatrice trembles from one motive – Alsemero attributes
  another.
bless Ironic.
That ... occasions Dramatic irony. See IV,2,36.
necessary Beatrice speaks with conscious irony.
Dog at Like a dog, i.e. keen.
should Could.
countenanced Favoured.
heavy Lazy.
And ... good However good they are.
virginity Synonym for 'maid' – but of course De Flores speaks
  ironically.
thing Person – who has now become a 'thing'.
woman Waiting-woman.
Are greedy of Greedily consume.
I charge ... us This remark might be expected to disturb Beatrice. In
  fact it gives her an excuse to end her acting.
raised Alarmed.
pains in't Risks about it.
double i.e. for both seeing the fire and putting it out. But Beatrice
  speaks with another meaning, signalling her distance from De Flores.
  See line 125 below.
call upon me i.e. for reward.
Precious Ingenious. Unclear whether this is a description or an
  address (to Beatrice).
bouts Contests.
sport i.e. sexual pleasure.

Act V Scene 2

While Tomazo is vowing to withdraw from the world in disgust,
De Flores passes across the stage and Tomazo feels an over-
whelming surge of distaste for the man he greeted warmly the
previous day. The two men exchange blows and De Flores
retreats in confusion. Vermandero enters, claiming to have discovered the culprits – Franciscus and Antonio – and Tomazo
leaves with him.

Commentary

In the usual revenge tragedy this would be the scene in which
the avenger makes his preparations to exact justice. Tomazo, in
contrast, decides on retreat – until he sees De Flores. In sharp
contrast to their previous encounter this one is savagely
antagonistic. Once again the irrational elements in the play

surface: Tomazo has no reason to hate De Flores but he can smell trouble – at least so De Flores himself thinks. This is a bad omen. The scene ends with a deliberate anti-climax – the discovery of the culprits by Vermandero, which allows a spectacular conclusion in the next scene, when Alsemero is able to reveal the true murderers and take control of the situation. Note how De Flores is already on the run – in marked contrast to his previous behaviour. He is happy only when taking the initiative – as his final act of suicide demonstrates.

in About.

all men The morally destructive quality of murder is here made plain. Not only is it a sin in itself: it destroys the bonds of trust between all men.

***Enter* DE FLORES** It is dramatically appropriate that he should enter at this moment.

hard bestead Hard put to it.

of a pest-house In a plague hospital.

contrariety Conflict.

that face Once again it is De Flores' looks which stir unease.

he loved i.e. one loved.

made account of Valued.

so … venomous i.e. De Flores.

go near to Virtually.

In … manhood Because the poisoning of the sword by De Flores's blood would give an unfair advantage to the user. Note the hyperbole of this speech, such strong feeling does De Flores stimulate.

politician Plotter, intriguer.

as in a crystal As though in a mirror.

this i.e. the sudden attack.

noble De Flores stresses the distance in birth between them, just as Beatrice did to him.

a wise lawyer Not like a soldier, who would fight back.

a favour A token. This mild response from the ruthless De Flores indicates the depth of his fear. Alonzo's ghost haunts him.

a subtler strain De Flores realizes that instinct has recourse to knowledge beyond the reason. Tomazo knows instinctively that De Flores is guilty, without actually having formulated the idea.

He … now He nearly discovered my secret then.

league Association – but also with the sense of 'loyalty to'.

not so … up I'll even restrain myself from common courtesy.

A brother may salute Which is just what Tomazo did in IV,2.

compliment Courtesy.

zeal Metonym for 'the information we gathered and which I bring with zeal.'

To … discoverers i.e. thank these men who will bring you peace.

that calm i.e. peace of mind resultant on knowing who the murderers are.
perfect Perform.
o'this hand In this way.
mine i.e. courtiers of mine.
habits Costumes, i.e. disguises.
abused in't Deceived in this.
my ... conduct My kindest of guides.
thirst See II,2,136.

Act V Scene 3

Alsemero and Jasperino have seen Beatrice and De Flores together in the garden; this has confirmed Jasperino's report (IV,2) that they are lovers. Beatrice enters and Alsemero challenges her with adultery. She replies by denying it and admitting to her part in Alonzo's murder, in order to prove her devotion to Alsemero. Horrified, he orders her into his private room. De Flores then enters and also admits to the murder. Alsemero puts him in the same room as Beatrice. When Vermandero comes in with all the other characters, announcing that he has arrested Antonio and Franciscus for the murder of Alonzo, Alsemero tells him that the real murderers are in the next room. Beatrice cries out, and De Flores brings her on stage, wounded. They admit to the crime and De Flores then stabs himself; Beatrice dies a few moments later. Antonio and Franciscus are cleared of any involvement, and Alibius resolves to behave better to his wife in future. The play ends with Alsemero's epilogue.

Commentary

Alsemero is only convinced of Beatrice's infidelity when he sees it – one of the many ironic uses of the eyesight theme in the play. The last scene has various examples of ignorance and knowledge, of which the most striking is Beatrice's belief that Alsemero will believe her denial of adultery if she admits to complicity in murder. Only at the very end – in classic fashion – does she achieve clear-sightedness about herself and her deeds. Her father too is violently brought to knowledge of the truth, and the dénouement in general is finely managed to bring about a whole series of revelations, even for the characters in the sub-plot who opportunely enter with Antonio and Franciscus to tie up the ends.

confidence i.e. in what Jasperino has told him about Beatrice and De Flores.

black mask i.e. Beatrice's dishonesty.

the face i.e. the face of sin.

despite to Despising of.

so . . . bottomless Apparently so endless.

Touch it home Probe it to the bottom.

She . . . opportunely She'll meet you conveniently (to be questioned).

None can so sure No one can do it so certainly.

honest Chaste.

brow Look, i.e. of Alsemero's.

strain Force.

vault i.e. of heaven.

Which i.e. laughing or crying.

faith Credence.

sadder colour i.e. if you cried it would look sadder, but it would still be a lie.

breath Word.

strikes Makes.

What . . . repair again The trust between them.

heart's rifling The examination of your heart (by Alsemero).

an easy passage i.e. there's nothing (like guilt) to obstruct you.

ground Cause.

tread on that Disdain it.

Unanswerable i.e. there is no shaming you. Compare V,1,126–7.

you . . . on i.e. it is a cause that gives no support to your claim to be chaste. As so often in the play, a word's meaning – in this case 'ground' – shifts and complicates the sense.

ticklish Lascivious.

visor Mask – of innocence. Compare V,3,3.

your despite The one you despised.

Lip's saint Both (1) the man you speak sweetly of, or to, and (2) the one who kisses you. He 'blesses' your lips and is constantly on them, as though he were your patron saint.

devil Both (1) evil spirit, and (2) drudge.

Your adultery Your (companion in) adultery.

counsel . . . bosom Your confidante.

Is . . . then? i.e. so much for your witness.

wages Consequences.

beguiled Deceived. Beatrice thinks she will excuse herself from suspicion of one crime by admitting another.

To . . . scandal From the sin of defiling your bed (with adultery).

stand up I defend my innocence.

a serpent i.e. De Flores.

temple See I,1,1.

'Twas in . . . See I,1,19–25.

'twill have it now The place will now have revenge.

bridge of blood Both (1) the murder of Alonzo, (2) the alliance with Alsemero.

I am true Even in this Beatrice lies – though she tells the truth about the murder.

charnel Sepulchre.

it must ask pause The bed itself must make me think.

yet Before this is finished.

put me in Given me a cue.

Commend Recommend. De Flores sustains the deceit.

since De Flores nearly gives himself away.

out i.e. washed out.

perceived A threat from Alsemero.

behindhand with Indebted to.

As ... to As certainly as death for.

And ... that She has also confessed much more.

It ... but It was bound to.

fair-faced See V,3,4.

crocodile Crocodile tears are proverbially hypocritical.

prey This follows from crocodile – but the significant implication is that Beatrice, not De Flores, is the main criminal.

pander Procurer, i.e. by putting them together.

black i.e. devilish.

Clip Embrace.

'tis the pilot She is the guide.

Mare Mortuum Dead Sea.

close Carefully.

Hear me Notice the rhetorical exchanges at 121–131.

nearer i.e. in relationship.

bandied Held up.

urgent in blood i.e. as a bloody deed, and in Tomazo's blood.

so stout yet Still strong enough.

broken rib i.e. Beatrice. The allusion is to Genesis II,21–23.

I am ... health Blood-letting for fever patients was a common practice.

upon't Upon it, i.e. upon your blood in me.

distinction Separate existence.

Beneath ... corruptible In Elizabethan cosmology the stars belonged to the eternal heavens above, meteors to the changeable world below the moon. Meteors thus indicated and were even thought to cause evil. The meteor here is De Flores.

it from him My fate from the meteor/De Flores.

my loathing ... rest The obsession of Beatrice's hatred for De Flores presaged the inevitable involvement of their fates.

cozened Cheated.

barley-brake A game involving couples.

heart The inclination of her heart.

honour's prize Chastity.

that token i.e. the wound he gave.

that record i.e. the heavenly book of good and bad deeds.
lose Forget.
behind ... life After death.
quit Acquitted.
what ... done i.e. been revealed.
my injuries Those who injured me.
loose i.e. from his body.
opacous Cloudy.
behind To come.

Epilogue

stay Stop.
dry Dry (the tears for).
it Sorrow.
rather On the contrary.
Your only smiles Only your – the audience's – smiles.

Revision questions on Act V

1 What theatrical tricks do the authors use in this Act, and to what effect?

2 Does Diaphanta deserve her fate?

3 Are we meant, in any way, to admire De Flores in this Act?

4 What do you make of Alsemero's last words in the Epilogue and what bearing do they have on the play?

5 Is the end of the play dramatically and/or morally satisfying?

Middleton's art in *The Changeling*
The characters

De Flores

She that in life and love refuses me
In death and shame my partner she shall be

A major theme of *The Changeling* is obsession – and the form it finds is sexual obsession. Of all the characters in the play De Flores embodies this theme with the greatest power, strangeness and complexity; for he is not only himself obsessive but also, like Beatrice, the cause of obsession in others. The extremity of his ugliness is a pointer to the extremity of his passions and the absolute absence of positive moral sense, which together create a pathological creature remarkable even in a literary age of pathological creatures. De Flores is another of those studies in evil at which the Jacobeans excelled, comparable with Iago in *Othello* and Ferdinand in *The Duchess of Malfi*; yet he is quite different from either, a unique dramatic figure.

Like the other characters of the main plot, he appears in the play's first scene, and the relationship between him and Beatrice is immediately sketched in by her abrupt responses to his statements:

De F. Lady, your father –
Beat.   Is in health, I hope.
De F. Your eye shall instantly instruct you, lady.
          He's coming hitherward.
Beat.   What needed then
          Your duteous preface?   (I,1,93–96)

De Flores's desire for Beatrice and her loathing of him are perfectly matched. Paradoxically, by being so violently opposed to each other from the outset, the two characters are united within the dramatic scheme of the play. Both are excessive in their passions as in their appearance and the effect they have on others: De Flores's repulsiveness and Beatrice's beauty are both out of the ordinary, even unnatural. For Beatrice, hatred constitutes a kind of intimacy: that even the thought of De Flores disgusts her so strongly suggests what an effect he has on her. Appropriately, the play contains images of poison and antidote, and of poisons that are themselves also antidotes. Desire and loathing, it seems, share this ambivalent quality; one can turn into the other.

In the first scene of Act I De Flores almost immediately announces his obsession. He puts his passion down to fate, and Beatrice's loathing to 'a peevish will'. Yet peevishness can be synonymous with perversity, which De Flores himself exhibits in good measure, declaring that he'll pursue Beatrice, however badly she treats him: 'If but to spite her anger . . .' (I,1,105). His will, as the play reveals, is stronger than hers, and we can view the development of the relationship between them – which is central to the play – as a battle of wills. In this sense De Flores's courtship of Beatrice is like a black parody of all the comic courtships in Jacobean drama in which the sex war is fought out and brought to a happy conclusion. This impression is confirmed at the end of I,1, when De Flores reasserts himself after the other characters have left:

> I know she hates me,
> Yet cannot choose but love her:
> No matter, if but to vex her, I'll haunt her still;
> Though I get nothing else, I'll have my will.   (I,1,234–237)

These lines are ironically prophetic. 'Will' here means 'way', but there is a strong undertone of the other meaning – 'sexual pleasure'. Out of context these lines might easily be part of a comedy. In context, they are deadly serious: De Flores gets exactly what he asks for in the last line, in both senses of the word 'will'. The true comedy, of course, is going on elsewhere in the play, in the house of Alibius. Yet there is a level on which De Flores, like Iago, really is comic, and this last speech reveals it. Not only has Beatrice disdainfully rejected the glove De Flores offers her: she also throws its pair to the floor in disgust. The gesture indicates not only contempt, but the physical distaste she feels for him – the sense that she could hardly bear to touch him (a feeling exactly reversed when she decides to use him in II,2,81). De Flores contemplates the space Beatrice vacates as she sweeps off the stage:

> Here's a favour come, with a mischief! Now I know
> She had rather wear my pelt tann'd in a pair
> Of dancing pumps, than I should thrust my fingers
> Into her sockets here . . .   (I,1,231–34)

The gross sexual innuendo of 'thrust my fingers/Into her sockets' abruptly sharpens our sense of the physical: Beatrice's disgust is more than matched by De Flores's aching lust. But there is also an ironic and acute sense of self-appraisal: De Flores's spitting out of 'pelt' and 'pair' and 'pumps' brings home to us that he has a clear view of his own situation, which is not blended with self-contempt. He has none of Iago's doubts or uncertainties; for example, he does not, like Ferdinand in *The Duchess of Malfi*, decline into madness. Clarity of vision, lack of self-pity and an indifference to everything but the fulfilment of his desires are all essential characteristics. Thus De Flores is able to contemplate the black humour of his situation – and, later, the situation of his victims – without the complication of subsidiary emotions. Almost his last words echo this first important speech:

> I thank life for nothing
> But that pleasure: it was so sweet to me
> That I have drunk up all, left none behind
> For any man to pledge me.   (V,3,168–171)

Thus can De Flores wittily express his possession of Beatrice's virginity within seconds of taking his own life, knowing full well that his shaft will hit home in Vermandero and Alsemero, who value virginity so highly. Again, the humour, black though it is, purges De Flores's departure of any hint of sentiment. Fulfilled desire feels no emotion but satisfaction, and in that sense De Flores can be said to have a kind of triumph. He dies, after all, a successful man.

Before that moment is reached we observe one of the most extraordinary relationships even in the morbid catalogue of Jacobean drama, as Beatrice moves from uncontrollable loathing of De Flores, through admiration to dependence. How does De Flores achieve his objective? Partly because he subordinates every other moral consideration to it; partly because, like Iago, he is a brilliant improviser; partly because he has the courage of a man with nothing to lose; and partly because of the other characters' simplicity. De Flores, after all, is an outsider: a servant in a world of masters, hideous in a play dominated by the attractive Beatrice and Alsemero. No one considers him, he is a part of the furniture. This is made very plain when, for example, he is loftily rewarded by all concerned after putting out the fire (V,1). But, caring nothing for his honour – unlike Vermandero, Tomazo and the rest – he can be indifferent to such treatment. Indeed, De Flores constitutes a kind of critique of the aristocratic notion of honour, still so crucially important in the early seventeenth century. In such a context, honour is to a man as chastity to a woman: something without which they cannot exist socially. But this code applies only to ladies and gentlemen: servants – such as Diaphanta – are cheerfully indifferent to this aristocratic preoccupation.

While De Flores claims to be of good descent, his status puts him in the same class as Diaphanta, and the class difference between him and Beatrice is a feature of the play. While she *uses* him like a servant, she fondly believes he will *behave* like a gentleman – and is shocked when he does not, but instead demands his reward in the form of her body. De Flores inverts the whole gentlemanly code by refusing to play according to the rules, a difference neatly expressed by the comparison between Alsemero's offer to challenge Alonzo and De Flores's simple disposal of him. Such ruthlessness is, of course, part of his appeal for Beatrice, suggesting how closely social and sexual attitudes are bound up in the play. The Piracquo brothers are the most concerned with honour – and Beatrice finds them least attractive. Alsemero is physically appealing, but passive beside the hideous and dynamic De Flores. De Flores is base but virile, and his virility cannot be distinguished from his baseness.

De Flores's behaviour thus expresses the truth that sexuality is potentially subversive of the social order – a common enough theme in the literature of the period: we need only think of the attractive and virile Edmund in *King Lear*, a man who causes the downfall of both Goneril and Regan. In that play base sexuality is associated with evil. In the person of Desdemona in *Othello*, chastity and submissiveness are equated with good. In *The Changeling* there is no equivalent to Desdemona: all the characters pursue their desires to a greater or lesser degree, even Alsemero. De Flores is simply the most extreme case of a general condition. *The Changeling* is quite without the cosmological scope of *King Lear*: like many non-Shakespearian Jacobean tragedies, it is a play in which the metaphysical dimension, the existence of Heaven and Hell and souls, seems to be purely formal, a metaphorical extension of this world. When De Flores says at the end 'now we are left in hell' the present tense is suggestive: despite the conventional references to eternal punishment, our sense of earthly existence and dissolution is too strong to leave much room for anything else. The drama is domestic, not philosophical. While the moral framework is relatively crude — the evil-doers are caught and punished — the psychological and emotional subtlety is considerable; and the focus for this is on Beatrice and De Flores.

The relevant scenes are II,2; III,4 and V,1. In II,2 Beatrice rejects Alsemero's proposal to challenge Alonzo and then thinks of De Flores as the right person to dispose of her unwanted suitor. De Flores accordingly enters, speculating on the frailty of women: once tempted, they will prostitute themselves to any man. Lollio too comforts himself with this conventional reflection (IV,3,35). As it happens, they are both wrong: Isabella does not fall and Beatrice only gives way against her will. The irony is that De Flores gets his desire though he acts on the basis of muddled principles. The scene's irony arises from misunderstanding: Beatrice thinks she will reward De Flores with money, while he is determined to have her.

In III,4, De Flores asserts his domination of Beatrice, and shows his contempt for her self-deceit, which is based on a sense of her own innate superiority. De Flores shows how crime has made them equals and inevitable partners. She gives way unwillingly, but in V,1, he completes his conquest by winning her admiration and respect for his daring. De Flores may be base by birth and hideous in appearance, but his natural gifts easily outshine Alsemero and Alonzo in her eyes, simply because they appear so readily to gratify her will.

Beatrice

Ever hung my fate 'mongst things corruptible.

According to the dictionary definition, a changeling can be 'one apt to change' — especially a woman. This gives the play's title a clear application to Beatrice, who changes her allegiance during its course: from Alonzo to Alsemero and from Alsemero to De Flores. We first meet her when she is in the process of discarding her betrothed for the attractive Alsemero, for whom she has experienced love at first sight. Their first conversation, like the opening exchanges between Alsemero and Jasperino, might be taken from a Jacobean comedy: light, learned, witty and aristocratic. In view of what happens, Beatrice appears surprisingly judicious: 'Our eyes are sentinels unto our judgments, / And should give certain judgment what they see (I,1,72–3), she says, in lines which come to take on an ironic ring. Beatrice's eyes betray her by admitting the image of the desirable Alsemero; judgement is precisely what she lacks. When she says, a few lines later, 'Sure, mine eyes were mistaken,' she is referring to Alonzo, whom she feels fate cannot have meant for her. Again this is ironic: 'fate' does have something very different and very terrible in store for her – not Alsemero, however, but the hated De Flores.

Beatrice's loathing of De Flores is sketched in with great economy: their first exchanges make his comment (I,1,100–107) almost superfluous, and lead to a crucial discussion of likes and dislikes between Beatrice and Alsemero. He makes the point that one man's meat is another man's poison, and when Beatrice asks him 'what may be your poison, sir?', the innocent question foreshadows the ironic answer given by the play: Beatrice herself. This outstandingly beautiful woman, who embodies the desires of three men in the play, turns out to be fatal to two of them and disastrous for the third: she is both meat and poison. Beatrice is not unaware of her own changeability: 'I shall change my saint, I fear me, I find / A giddy turning in me ... (I,1,155–6),' she says. Nor does she discount the strangeness of her violent loathing for De Flores. But overall she remains unreflective, quite unable to calculate the consequences of her actions or the moral implications of her shifting desires. Cut free from the constraints of conventional moral standards she is at sea, acting on impulse and moving from moment to moment. In this respect her uncontrollable dislike of De Flores is a sign of a more fundamental malaise, for Beatrice is dominated by her desires. The pervasive 'sight' imagery also hints at this: for Beatrice there is no real gap between seeing something she wants and reaching for it – anything which gets in the way, such as a man's life, is hardly worth noticing. Beatrice, in fact, has no imagination: she has to see something in order to appreciate its reality. It is only when De Flores produces Alonzo's severed finger that she becomes at all conscious of the enormity of the murder. Even then her horror is soon dismissed with a request that De Flores bury the finger and keep the ring.

Self-absorbed as she is, Beatrice dominates the play through her relationships with the men in it: Vermandero, Alonzo,

Tomazo, Alsemero, Jasperino and De Flores are all affected by her in different ways – and, in their turn, affect her. To her father she is an appendage, to be disposed of to the most suitable person. This she knows and resents: 'His blessing / Is only mine, as I regard his name . . .' (II,1,20–21).

Vermandero is appropriately punished for his blindness in his most tender spot: his honour, as it is embodied in Beatrice's chastity. Alonzo, too, is blind, and suffers accordingly: Beatrice's beauty can close men's eyes to her faults, as Alsemero discovers in time. Tomazo and Jasperino represent a sharper view of things: their vision is unclouded by love or desire. The fascination of De Flores results from the fact that he is both obsessed with Beatrice and yet realistic about her: he sees her weakness but he desires her beauty. Her haughtiness only excites him the more, because it expresses not strength but vulnerability, as she admits:

I never see this fellow, but I think
Of some harm towards me, danger's in my mind still;
I scarce leave trembling of an hour after.   (II,1,89–91)

Whether positively or negatively, Beatrice's life is dominated by sexuality – desire and loathing. Though she puts her initial loathing of De Flores down to physical disgust, once he has impressed her it becomes clear that this was, if a reason, only a partial one. What she responds to so violently is his desire for her, which entirely lacks the gentlemanly restraint of Alonzo or the graceful beauty of Alsemero. De Flores's desire is lust pure and simple, the lust of the Beast for Beauty.

This is, of course, to see the play in traditional terms, and there is a rather different view we might take of it in which Beatrice figures as a kind of heroine or anti-heroine. This view depends upon seeing her as a rebel against all the constrictions of parents, conventional marriage, the role of women, obligatory virtue and passivity. Looked at this way, Beatrice can emerge as a kind of heroic revolutionary: 'If there were none such name as Piracquo, / Nor no such tie as the command of parents!' (II,2,20–21) rings out as a cry from the heart. Sexual freedom, in this interpretation, stands for a larger kind of freedom in a world where women are not ground down by the demands of men. As things stand, Beatrice is used by her father and her various lovers to satisfy their lust or their ideas of honour. Her violent response and her indifference to their sufferings can be seen to represent rejection of a society in which women are pawns and their desires incidental to the purposes of the menfolk.

If this view *is* taken, it is possible to make more sense of an apparent contradiction in the play, namely the conflict between Beatrice's apparent sensuousness and her extreme reluctance to consummate her sexual relationships. In both cases of postponement, of course, there are good plot reasons for this – though it is hard to see what difference postponement can make to Alonzo's ultimate fate. The whole thing makes a little more sense if we see Beatrice's virginity as one of the two weapons she has to fight her battles in a male-dominated society. The other is her beauty. Both are double-edged, for both produce just the result she wishes to avoid. On the other hand, they bring her the desire of the man she wants, Alsemero. The point here is that what Beatrice really wants is freedom, freedom to choose; and this is expressed in the desire for freedom to love where she will. Put like this we can see the play as a conflict between the conventional – Vermandero, the Piracquo brothers and perhaps Alsemero – and the rebels: De Flores and Beatrice.

That this interpretation of the play is by no means a fanciful one becomes clear when we remember that Jacobean playwrights, including Shakespeare, were preoccupied with the social and sexual situation of women, and that this was an explosive topic in the early seventeenth century, a period in which the High Renaissance emphasis on the 'masculine' virtues of action and reason was displaced by a 'feminine' interest in feeling and introspection. The characteristically virtuous heroines of late Tudor drama give way to a series of complex, sensuous women: the Duchess of Malfi and Vittoria (Webster), Bianca and Beatrice (Middleton), Cleopatra (Shakespeare) and Annabella (Ford) are among them. Such women, like Beatrice, appear to be at odds with the conventional demands of society, the victims of their own irrational sensuality. This is not to 'excuse' their misdeeds – merely to suggest that they can only be fully understood in the larger context, unconditioned by purely male values.

Alsemero

He does ill, to tempt your sight, if he knew it.

Alsemero is a nobleman, a traveller, a dabbler in magic. All these things are important, but they pale into insignificance beside the central fact about him: that his habitual indifference to women is transformed by the sight of Beatrice into a passion for her so strong that he will only believe in her unfaithfulness when he has the evidence of his own eyes. Thus Alsemero's main role in the play is to testify to the power of Beatrice's attraction in particular, and sexual desire in general. The play opens with this very point. Alsemero enters, meditating on his meeting with Beatrice in the church, a place which seems to sanctify their mutual love. This irony is compounded by Alsemero's reference to omens and his observing: 'The temple's vane to turn full in my face;' (I,1,20). In contrast to Alsemero's rhapsodic passion, the scene is coloured by such images of doubt – the gale (17), the hidden malady (24), the smoke and fire (50). Yet Alsemero, in response to Jasperino's ironic question about his changed intentions, claims that, 'I keep the same church, same devotion.' (35), and this conflict of uncertainty and obstinacy gives a key not only to Alsemero's predicament but to a major aspect of the play, which explores the dangerous paradox of sexual passions: that they are over-whelmingly strong, yet prey to the smallest chance of cir-cumstance. This disparity between causes and effects is at the heart of the play's irony. As the more realistic Jasperino puts it: 'The laws of the Medes are chang'd' (58). His own encounter with Diaphanta a few moments later is on a very different level, and the contrast between the two liaisons is maintained throughout the play. Jasperino's 'normal' and slightly coarse response to Diaphanta points up Alsemero's lofty idealism.

Yet if Beatrice's beauty entices Alsemero, it is made plain that he too is more than usually attractive. Alsemero, in fact, corresponds to the conventional hero: handsome, aristocratic, chivalrous and pure-minded. He is perhaps also a little simple-minded, responding to Beatrice's complaints about her betrothal by offering to challenge Alonzo to a duel, then showing no sign of surprise when the former suitor con-veniently disappears. This lack of curiosity results primarily from a need not to over-complicate the plot, but it fits in well with Alsemero's high-mindedness and with his infatuation. He is hypnotized by Beatrice: even when the trusted Jasperino produces damning evidence against her, she has only to enter for her power over Alsemero to be re-established (IV,2,125). In a play obsessed with images of vision, the mere sight of Beatrice is enough to reassure him – as it is enough to stir the passions of her other admirers, Alonzo and De Flores. In Alsemero's case it can unsettle the regular habits of a lifetime and make a confirmed traveller (I,1,26–32) into a stay-at-home.

To all appearances the two make a fine couple, yet their moral separation is apparent almost from the start; Beatrice understands instinctively that she can neither ask Alsemero to do what De Flores does, nor trust him with the knowledge of the deed. Unlike Beatrice, Alsemero will never let his lust outrun his sense of honour. In this respect, too, he resembles the conventional hero, embodying the traditional moral standards within which the play works. In this sense his heroism is indeed muted, a pale thing compared with the reckless adventures of De Flores. The comparison serves to remind us of the different ways in which the word 'hero' may be used. Jacobean drama has its share of virtuous protagonists but they commonly act as foils to more complex characters. *The Changeling* is a case in point. The comparison between Alonzo, Alsemero and De Flores is natural and instructive.

Isabella and Diaphanta

Does love turn fool, run mad, and all at once?

I shall carry't well
Because I love the burthen.

Isabella

While Isabella remains undeveloped as a character, she has a vital role to play as a foil for Beatrice, remaining constant and virtuous where her social superior gives way to desire.

The familiar situation of the young wife to an old husband is mildly complicated by making Alibius the superintendent of an asylum – though this is by no means unique in Jacobean drama. The intrigue involving Isabella demands that she, like Beatrice, must be sexually attractive; and the comedy derives in part from her resistance to the advances made by Franciscus and Antonio, and the fun she has at their expense. It is this which generates irony – for the usual outcome of such a situation is the deception of the elderly husband in favour of a young lover. In *The Changeling* it is the lovers who are made to look foolish, not the husband. And the irony is heightened by the natural comparison between Isabella and Beatrice. Alsemero is deceived and betrayed, while Alibius escapes with a mild rebuke. Beatrice is completely dominated by the need to satisfy her desires, while Isabella has herself well under control. Beatrice is emotional, Isabella is rational. Beatrice is destroyed, Isabella survives and triumphs. The contrast is even made clear in the behaviour of the two women. Beatrice is constantly carried along by events, to the point where she becomes, as De Flores puts it, 'the deed's creature'. In Isabella's case, she is the one who acts decisively, to put an end to the intrigue in the madhouse. Beatrice is passive, Isabella active.

Diaphanta
The character of Diaphanta adds a third level of female interest to the play; the three women are complementary in their attitudes. Both Beatrice and Diaphanta have strong sexual appetites, but Beatrice's is dressed up in the language of love whereas her maid talks about pleasure. Both are betrayed by their desires. Like Isabella, Diaphanta is not developed as a character. Instead she plays a stock role: the knowing, easy-going, practical servant, who comes to grief through no major fault of her own, but through a weakness of the flesh: she cannot tear herself away from the pleasures of Alsemero's love-making. Just as Isabella provides one kind of foil for Beatrice, Diaphanta provides another, and her fate echoes her mistress's – just as her relationship with Jasperino parallels that of Beatrice with Alsemero.

Vermandero

I tell thee, knave, mine honour is in question.

Beatrice's father stands for order, tradition, loyalty, honour and all the military virtues against which Beatrice and De Flores so flagrantly sin. His first appearance makes this clear. A conversation reveals that Alsemero is the son of John de Alsemero, a comrade in arms of Vermandero (I,1) and this gives rise to memories of old campaigns. Yet Vermandero is also warm-hearted and impulsive. He remembers Alsemero's father with affection; and he says of Alonzo: 'I would not change him for a son-in-law / For any he in Spain, the proudest he ...' (I,1,215–16).

But it is the combination of traditionalism and emotion that proves fatal to Vermandero's insight – for this combination is what characterizes his attitude to Beatrice. He loves his daughter, even dotes on her. When she requests a delay in the marriage with Alonzo, Vermandero agrees – 'It is but reasonable' (II,1,112). And when Alonzo, as he believes, deserts Beatrice on her wedding-day he is outraged: (He) 'mock'd my daughter's joy; the prepar'd morning / Blush'd at his infidelity ...' (IV,2,27–8). However, this love is inseparable from an acute sense of his own honour: the lines quoted above follow Vermandero's claim that Alonzo 'Has too much marr'd both my abused love, / The honourable love I reserved for him ...' (25–6).

Throughout the play his attitude to Beatrice is bound up with his sense of proper social conventions and the respect due to his own name. Beatrice herself is well aware of this, and shows signs of rebelling against it. She acknowledges that her father has always called her his 'best love' (I,1,172) – but later, when contemptuously dismissing the idea of marriage with Alonzo, she says:

> what's Piracquo
> My father spends his breath for? And his blessing
> Is only mine, as I regard his name,
> Else it goes from me, and turns head against me,
> Transform'd into a curse ...   (II,1,19–23)

Here, using the play's characteristic imagery of opposites, of one thing turning into another, Beatrice accurately expresses the truth. Her analysis is exactly borne out by Vermandero's final comment in the play: 'Oh, my name is enter'd now in that record / Where till this fatal hour 'twas never read' (V,3,180–81). Vermandero thinks not of his daughter but of his honour. Like the other men in the play he sees Beatrice as a means to his own end, an adjunct to himself. Throughout he has noticed nothing about her reactions – in the way, for instance, that Tomazo notices her indifference to his brother. Vermendero's doting has been a form of self-indulgence, of laziness. He is not a bad man, but he is a man and, as such, unaware of his daughter as a woman with passions and desires of her own. In this sense, he is also very much a father – not a bad father, but a selfish one.

Vermandero is, of course, largely a stock character: Jacobean drama is full of self-important touchy old men who are fooled by their daughters. And it is as a stock character that he has his importance in the play. The case of Alibius is exactly parallel. Though the doctor is a husband, not a father, he is a busy, amiable self-important man who talks to his wife about his affection for her: 'In my arms and bosom, my sweet Isabella, / I'll lock thee up most nearly' (III,3,249–50). In practice he ignores her: 'Lollio, / We have employment . . .' (III,3,250–51). It is left to Isabella to bring him to his senses, just as Beatrice's fate shocks her father – though not, alas, into his. Alibius has a chance to 'reform' not available to Vermandero. This is the difference between the comic and the tragic modes.

Alonzo and Tomazo de Piracquo

Thou art so exceptious still.

I tell you, sir, the gentleman's complete.

Alonzo

The two brothers are contrasted. Alonzo is trusting, warm, open, enthusiastic and blind; in the end he becomes a victim. Tomazo is shrewd, suspicious, passionate, vengeful and perceptive; he takes on the role of the pursuing avenger, though he presides over the final act of justice rather than meting it out. Only Alonzo is really necessary to the plot, as the cause of Beatrice's first link with De Flores. He is enthusiastically characterized by Vermandero:

I tell you, sir, the gentleman's complete,
A courtier and a gallant, enrich'd
With many fair and noble ornaments . . .   (I,1,212–14).

And so he proves to be, politely acceding to Beatrice's request to delay the wedding and refusing to listen to any breath of criticism against her, even from his brother. He suffers from what Tomazo calls 'love's tame madness' (II,2,154), and idealizes Beatrice, just as Alsemero is to do. This proves his downfall. Like her father, he is wilfully blind to the true nature of Beatrice's feelings, and pays the price accordingly.

Tomazo

Tomazo, on the other hand, notices Beatrice's indifference to his brother. Untouched by her beauty, he is prepared to assess the evidence of her demeanour and her request to postpone the wedding. Tomazo's criticism Alonzo writes off as trivial: 'Fie, you are too severe a censurer / Of love in all points ...' (II,1,107–8); and he is annoyed by Tomazo's hint that such a woman will soon transfer her affection to any number of men, and so dishonour his name. This point about women – that those who change once will change many times – crops up several times in the play: both Lollio and De Flores light on it as encouragement for their suits; and the different attitudes of the brothers epitomize different male attitudes to women. Tomazo is suspicious, wary; Alonzo is trusting, idealistic. They have their counterparts in Jasperino and Alsemero.

After Alonzo's death, Tomazo and the ghost share a role, providing a constant reminder of imminent divine vengeance. Both of them ultimately point to De Flores as the culprit, the ghost in the 'Dumb Show' and V,1, and Tomazo in his extraordinary reversal of attitude to De Flores, from benevolence to violent instinctive dislike (V,2). Tomazo's expression of disillusion with life in this scene and his description of De Flores are very characteristic of Jacobean melancholy: that sickness of the soul which arises from impotence and which is acutely sensitive to the disgusting and repellent. Because Tomazo cannot identify the murderer he is suspicious of all men, and this makes him weary of life. As he reflects on this state of affairs, De Flores crosses the stage, bringing Tomazo's general reflections into focus. The man's ugliness is at odds with his reputation for honesty. He seems to poison everything around him. In an extraordinary outburst Tomazo declares that:

He would go near to poison any weapon
That should draw blood on him; one must resolve
Never to use that sword again in fight,
In way of honest manhood, that strikes him;
Some river must devour it, 'twere not fit
That any man should find it. – What, again?

Enter DE FLORES
He walks a'purpose by, sure, to choke me up,
To infect my blood.   (V,2,18–25)

I have quoted this passage at some length because extended speeches and soliloquies are relatively rare in the play. When they occur, the reasons are very positive. These lines contribute to the atmosphere of horror in the last act by developing the poison-image that runs all the way through the play, and making it quite clear that this image is primarily associated with De Flores. In Act II Beatrice had spoken of De Flores as a poison (II,2,47) and now Tomazo's violent dislike for him echoes Beatrice's own revulsion. But it also points up just how far Beatrice has moved away from that revulsion, almost to love. This is typical of Tomazo's role as a background character, a maintainer of normal standards and sharp perceptions in the play. Like Jasperino he stands for common sense, for realism and decency. In the end he takes no part in the working out of justice, but stands by as a witness to it.

Lollio

I'll have my fool's part with you.

The play is full of pairs and comparisons: Alsemero and Jasperino with Alonzo and Tomazo, Beatrice with Isabella, Vermandero with Alibius. So it is natural to regard Lollio as the benign counterpart of the malevolent De Flores. Like him, Lollio is a servant in the house of an attractive woman, and again like De Flores Lollio is spurred on to make love to his mistress by the belief that a woman who listens to one lover will listen to any. Like De Flores, Lollio is a fixer, a manager: he helps Isabella just as De Flores 'helps' Beatrice. Like De Flores, Lollio is, after his fashion, sharp and witty, with a good eye for the weaknesses of others. But unlike De Flores, Lollio is also a bit of a fool, a fitting keeper for the asylum and for his master Alibius; Isabella is brighter than either of them. And unlike De Flores, Lollio hardly has serious designs on his mistress's virtue: she is, anyway, well able to look after herself.

The role of the comic servant is a popular one in Jacobean drama; to that extent Lollio, like the other subordinate figures in *The Changeling*, is a stock character. His comic exchanges sometimes sink to a very low level of invention, and he is not individualized. Instead he embodies a number of qualities: comically feeble lust, incompetence, low cunning, a taste for practical jokes, occasional bawdy and simple good humour. In these respects he contrasts markedly with De Flores, who is magnificently developed as a person.

Themes and structure

Themes

N. W. Bawcutt has suggested that *The Changeling* is 'basically a study in sin and retribution, expressed in terms of sexual relationships', and this is both an economical way of describing the play and an opening wide of the gates to interpretation; for many late Jacobean plays might well be described in the same terms. Perhaps the singular thing about *The Changeling* is the intensity with which it pursues this theme. Everything in the play is subordinated to the plot and its parallel sub-plot, both of which hang on comparable sexual intrigues, reflecting on one another. All other themes are subsidiary to this central preoccupation: the exploration of desire and its consequences. Desire, of course, comes in a variety of forms from the crudest lust to the most refined romantic love. The top end of this range is only just represented in the play, by Alonzo's touching faith in Beatrice. The writers are careful to show him trusting her absolutely, against the explicit advice of his brother; Alonzo's love can be seen more or less to transcend desire in its tragic idealizing of an unworthy object.

Compared with Alonzo, even Alsemero is seen to have his doubts, infatuated though he is; the virgin-testing potion bears witness to this. Yet Alsemero's 'love at first sight' expresses the loftiness of his desire and the power of Beatrice's beauty to transform the greatest misogynist. That Alsemero has never before shown an interest in women testifies to his immunity from mere lust: we are to understand that when he loves, his love is the real thing. The passionate desire he manifests for Beatrice on the wedding night (not knowing, of course, that her place has been taken by Diaphanta) combines with his previous indifference to make the point powerfully: that there is a vital distinction between lust and the legitimate desire sanctified by marriage.

It is this distinction which Beatrice's third admirer, De Flores, ignores. Like the other two, he is overwhelmed by her beauty but his feelings are directly translated into the longing to possess her at whatever cost, once the opportunity presents itself. Yet unlike the other two men, he is not blind to her nature: on the contrary, his calculations depend on the cynical assumption that a woman who will betray one man will betray many. He may be right, but it is ironic that Beatrice really does want only Alsemero, and sleeps with De Flores against her will. Yet once she gives way to him, the transforming power of desire becomes mutual: just as her beauty drew him like a magnet, so she is able to ignore his ugliness in her admiration and even love for a man who can plan and act so boldly. If the three men span the range of desire from the idealizing to the realistic, Beatrice can be said to comprehend all varieties because she is able to deceive herself, just as her first suitor and her husband are deceived. Beatrice *thinks* she is acting from love for Alsemero: at the end of the play, when justifying herself to him, she states this motive. Yet just as the desire her own beauty creates in men makes us question its nature and its value, so the desire Alsemero's beauty creates in her makes us repeat those questions. Sexual attraction is seen as potentially disruptive and dangerous, adept at disguising its own motives in the clothes of love. Beatrice's ability to ignore everything but her own wants gives a vivid demonstration of this.

Highlighting the exploration of desire in the main tragic plot, is the comic presentation of it in the sub-plot where, once again, three men pursue one woman. Isabella, unlike Beatrice, is already married and has her own feelings well under control. Antonio and Franciscus pretend to be mad in order to pursue her, while the mundane Lollio has his own plans. The parallels with the main plot are clear: Lollio, like De Flores, is a realist; the other two express themselves in parodies of 'poetic' language which hint at a satire on the romantic love of Alsemero and Alonzo. Isabella's beauty, like Beatrice's, provokes the action, but instead of pursuing her own desires, Isabella mocks the foolishness of the pseudo-madmen. She is not averse to adventures — would like to get out of the house — but has seen too many fools to become one herself. Desire, in fact, makes a fool or a madman of many other characters — Alsemero, Alonzo, De Flores, Beatrice — but not of Isabella. This is seen most pathetically in the case of Diaphanta. Unlike Beatrice in her worldly sensuality and unlike Isabella in her lack of restraint, Diaphanta's determination to enjoy herself and her blindness to any evil consequences reflect Beatrice's own recklessness. Diaphanta is, as it were, the polar opposite in her attitudes to Alsemero — a cheerful cynic who takes what she can get. Where desires conflict, one must give way to the other, it seems; and where desires conflict with the conventional moral order they must, in the end, pay the price. Sin is followed by retribution.

As usual in the better Jacobean drama, justice is by no means even-handed: the innocent sometimes perish with the guilty. Alonzo suffers for his blindness to the true nature of Beatrice's feelings, Diaphanta for her excessive lust. Yet in every case, the character's fate is not something arbitrarily imposed from outside, but follows as a consequence from his or her actions, and, as Bawcutt suggests, all these actions are sexual. Except for Vermandero, every major character is involved in sexual intrigue – and even his interference in Beatrice's marriage plans may be said to constitute a kind of involvement. Sexual relations become a particular case of general human relations, intensified by the violent eruption of irrationality. Desire is the thing over which people have little control: it needs great strength of will to resist – and in this play 'will' itself is a synonym for desire. The play expresses the conflict between desire and self-control in terms of 'love' and 'judgement'. Judgement is a combination of restraint and assessment. Isabella has it; Alsemero has it to some degree; Beatrice lacks it entirely; and to De Flores it is irrelevant. In *King Lear* Shakespeare makes the same equation between lust and injustice in the characters of Regan and Goneril: Edmund is their De Flores – a man who will do anything for what he wants, and who is the more attractive because of that. But in Shakespeare's play the behaviour of these characters is only one aspect of a larger injustice, created by Lear's foolishness. In *The Changeling* we concentrate on the central drama, and it gains accordingly in intensity.

Structure

The play is comparatively simple in structure. Although the main plot has elements of Revenge Tragedy – Tomazo eventually finds satisfaction in the punishment of his brother's killers – it is closer in spirit to Domestic Tragedy. This form, as the name suggests, concentrates on private relationships, especially adultery. The plot of *The Changeling* boils down to Beatrice's desire to rid herself of one suitor in favour of another, and the consequences that follow her achievement of this objective. The sub-plot involves Isabella's refusal to take a lover. Thus while the two plots are parallel, they also mirror each other: Beatrice falls, Isabella does not.

The play demonstrates a number of symmetries. The Isabella/Alibius/Lollio triangle reflects the relationship between Beatrice, Alsemero and De Flores, while not corresponding closely at all points. The important aspects of the comparison concern the ignorant husband, the adventurous wife and the knowing servant. The different resolutions of the two plots help to point up Beatrice's tragedy. She and De Flores are in every way more extreme than Isabella and Lollio, and their fate is correspondingly more serious. Beatrice's own behaviour is also symmetrical: at the beginning of the play she discards Alonzo in favour of Alsemero, and towards the end she appears to transfer her affection from Alsemero to De Flores. Just as she is first struck by Alsemero's attractiveness, so she is later overwhelmed by the virile character of De Flores. In one sense of the word, Beatrice herself is the changeling of the play's title, again in contrast with Isabella. The sub-plot also shows a symmetrical patterning, balancing Antonio and Franciscus against each other, for example; while the whole play is concerned with various pairs of lovers, some serious, some not: Beatrice and Alonzo, Beatrice and Alsemero, Beatrice and De Flores, Jasperino and Diaphanta, Diaphanta and Alsemero, Isabella and Franciscus, Isabella and Antonio. The interlocking of these various combinations supports the two plots and reinforces the obsessive theme of sexual desire.

Just as the main plot has elements of Revenge Tragedy and Domestic Tragedy, so the sub-plot bears some resemblance to the anti-masques common at the time. The masque is a serious and highly artificial dramatic form in which an abstract idea, such as virtue or wisdom, is dramatized in a series of tableaux involving words, music, mime and dance. It often involves, also, a kind of self-parody in which the serious subject is comically treated: this is the anti-masque. To the extent that the sub-plot is a comic variant on the main plot, it can be classified in this way – thus justifying a part of the play which might otherwise seem irrelevant. Some critics (notably Una Ellis Fermor in *The Jacobean Drama*) have suggested that *The Changeling* would be improved by omitting the sub-plot, leaving the intense economy of the main action to speak for itself. On the other hand, the mixture of comedy and tragedy is highly typical of the period and gives this play, among many others, its characteristic flavour. The comedy, as it were, heightens the horror by juxtaposing the ordinary world against the almost dream-like evil of De Flores and Beatrice — and the contrast is made the more ironic because the sub-plot takes place in a madhouse, while the real madness develops in Vermandero's castle.

If the mixture of comedy and tragedy is typical of the period, the same can be said of the various structural devices used in the play. The Dumb Show at the beginning of Act IV, for example, can be matched by a similar scene in *The Duchess of Malfi* written ten years earlier by one of Middleton's other collaborators, Webster. The Dumb Show is not only intrinsic to the plot: it serves to convey a good deal of action economically and graphically, while adding variety and piquancy to the play. The appearance of the ghost, who crops up in the Dumb Show and at the beginning of Act V, is another common device, again an economical and vivid way of expressing the imminence of divine vengeance. The obvious parallel here is with the ghost of the dead king in *Hamlet*. Alonzo's ghost does not speak, but his appearance is eloquent enough.

One unusual and sensational aspect of the play, in which it differs from normal Revenge Tragedy, concerns the death of the villain. De Flores commits suicide. There is a parallel for this at the end of *Othello* when the Moor falls on his own sword; but in earlier Revenge Tragedy the precendent was for the avenger — in this case it would have been Tomazo — to do the killing, thus achieving the justice of personal vengeance. De Flores's suicide is a final expression of his wilfulness, his refusal to be governed by others, for all his servile status, and it adds to our sense of his heroic stature. Or perhaps one should say anti-heroic stature — for the most interesting aspect of the play's structure is that, while justice is done at the end, the virtuous characters remain comparatively unsympathetic, or dull. The two interesting central characters — De Flores and Beatrice — move from nominal virtue to a full acceptance of their evil.

The heroically wicked protagonist is by no means an invention of Middleton and Rowley: Marlowe used similar figures, and Shakespeare's Iago is comparable. But nowhere else do we find such an exultant affirmation of triumph as in De Flores's last speeches. Even Milton's Satan in *Paradise Lost* comes to grief and is humiliated. But in contrast to Beatrice's self-abnegation: 'Let the common sewer take [me] from distinction' (V,3,153), De Flores's sneering insistence on his 'theft' of Beatrice's virginity rings out defiantly. During the course of the play this character moves from the periphery of the action to the centre, displacing his social superiors, and scoring a kind of moral victory over them. While this is in no way endorsed by the authors, what one might call the 'interest factor' means that we pay more attention to De Flores – like him or not – than to any other character except Beatrice. Thus the structure of the play – the way in which the action and the imagery increasingly move De Flores to the foreground – is at odds with the conventional morality that provides the background.

Style

As one of the better Jacobean tragedies, *The Changeling* exhibits a combination of economy and intensity in its language to which we are accustomed in the work of Shakespeare, Jonson and Webster. The relatively narrow range of imagery and the frequent recurrence of certain master concepts contribute to this intensity, which is appropriate to the morbid, nerve-wracking quality of the central action. In contrast, the language of the sub-plot has a colloquial richness, sometimes descending into bathos, with which we are also familiar from the great comedies of the period. It is certainly true that in plays such as *King Lear*, *Hamlet* and *The Duchess of Malfi* we find greater linguistic richness and variety, but *The Changeling* compensates for its limitations in this respect by an energetic forward movement and sinewy outline which are instantly imprinted on the mind. Like *Othello*, this is very much an inward drama: our concern is with psychology, with the workings of diseased hearts and minds; and like that play *The Changeling* contains a number of remarkably powerful scenes in which the pith of the inward action is concentrated – notably II,2 and III,4.

There are two basic modes – the dignified and the farcical. For the most part, plot and sub-plot are distinguished accordingly, until the last scene when they meet. But within the basic dignity of the tragic scenes we find a wide range of tone: from Alsemero's rhapsodic opening lines to Tomazo's haughty anger; from the intricate word-play of Beatrice's first discussion with her husband-to-be, to De Flores's measured glee in his evil deeds and his conquest of Beatrice. While they lack a comparable range of effects, the comic scenes also demonstrate some variety, moving from farce to verbal comedy, even touching, at moments, on a kind of dignity in Isabella's response to her two ridiculous lovers. The tragic and comic modes are sharply contrasted. Prose, for example, is used almost entirely for the comic scenes, reserving the greater dignity of long verse passages for the tragic action. The comic scenes, as one might expect, employ a racy colloquialism foreign to the tragedy; although it is true that the often complex speeches of De Flores show a greater linguistic range than the speeches of other characters. This is appropriate, for De Flores is suspended between the play's two worlds of masters and servants, aristocrats and bourgeois. The tragic scenes on the other hand, touch heights of lyricism quite beyond the comic plot.

Rhetoric

Sharp though these differences are, both modes make play with the kind of rhetorical devices to which Elizabethan and Jacobean writers were much given. Take, for example, the first conversation of Beatrice and Alsemero (I,1,64–86). After some preliminary compliments, in which love is characteristically compared to music, both the speakers make what amount to formal statements in which the notion of judgement plays a vital part:

Bea. Our eyes are sentinels unto our judgments,
     And should give certain judgment what they see:
     But they are rash sometimes, and tell us wonders
     Of common things, which when our judgments find,
     They can then check the eyes and call them blind.

The triple use of 'judgment', which we today find clumsy, is deliberate: the speech elaborates on the conceit – or metaphor – in which the eyes are supposed to guard the judgement – and it is, of course, ironic: judgement is what Beatrice completely lacks, and her eyes are what betray her, by making her vulnerable to Alsemero's charms. The insistence on the conceit fixes it in the mind: when, some time later, Beatrice reflects that Alsemero has chosen his friend Jasperino 'with judgment' – which makes her all the wiser in choosing him – and when she then concludes that 'I love now with the eyes of judgment' (II,1,7 and 13), we are alert to the ironic implications of her fatuous self-confidence. And to preclude any chance of the audience's missing the point, the authors make Alsemero reply to Beatrice in Act I in the same vein:

But I am further, lady; yesterday
Was mine eyes employment, and hither now
They brought my judgment, where are both agreed   (I,1,77–9).

Alsemero too is sadly deluded: he too is betrayed by the evidence of his eyes. Both characters ignore the power of love and desire to overthrow the judgement. Notice also how Alsemero's reply carefully takes up Beatrice's words and elaborates on them – 'But I am *further*, lady.' This patterning is fundamental to the literature of the period, and often the result of a formal education based on close analysis of rhetoric in classical literature, which codified literary techniques in terms of their effectiveness, considering drama very much as we consider journalism or legal argument, i.e. as a matter of carefully marshalling the most persuasive arguments. Thus speeches in a play are not merely a matter of direct expression: they are carefully designed to do a particular job, or several jobs. In the case of the example quoted above, not only is the developing relationship between Alsemero and Beatrice presented, but its tragic development is fore-shadowed, one of the play's themes is presented – the effect of desire on judgement – and an ironic point is made.

We can find a comic equivalent of this in the sometimes wearisome exploitation of the jokes about fools and madmen. In I,2, for example, Lollio explains that:

We have but two sorts of people in the house, and both under the whip, that's fools and madmen; the one has not wit enough to be knaves, and the other not knavery enough to be fools. (lines 44–47)

The punning on 'fool' (simpleton/dupe) figures throughout Lollio's part, referring to the deceptions of Antonio and Franciscus, who not only pretend to be fools (simpletons) in order to make love to Isabella, but really are fools (dupes) for that reason. Love has 'made a fool' of each of them. As it happens, this point links with the earlier one I made about Beatrice and Alsemero, i.e. that desire undermines their judgement. So the rhetorical patterns made in the language can be seen to relate to the larger structural pattern of the play, in this and other respects.

Pattern

The verbal patterning of the play is remarkably tightly-knit, Take, for example, the hint given in the title: a changeling is, among other things, a changeable person. The play's opening lines immediately hint at change: Alsemero has met someone and fallen in love with her, but it both pleases and worries him. He refers to omens: the weather vane is against him (line 20); he may have a hidden malady (line 24). His servants notice (line 50) and Jasperino comments that: 'The laws of the Medes are chang'd sure, salute / a woman! (58). Alsemero is disturbed but resolute: 'I keep the same church, same devotion' (35), he says, in a line which hints at just the opposite; for it is in church he has met Beatrice – and the church weather-vane is against him. Sure enough, Beatrice herself takes up a similar image when, questioned by her father, she says to herself: 'I shall change my saint, I fear me, I find / A giddy turning in me . . .' (155–6)

Later, Alsemero changes his mind about accepting Vermandero's invitation: 'Not chang'd so soon, I hope?' (201) asks his host, and it seems that Alsemero has become as changeable as Beatrice herself: desire unsettles everything. Appropriately, the scene ends with De Flores's insistence that he, at least, will not change – and this remains the case throughout the play. For the other characters this is not the case.

One might say that Beatrice remains constant in her changeability – but this paradox is belied at the end of the play, when she at last accepts her condition as the proper partner of De Flores. After Beatrice's death, the theme of change is made explicit in a passage (V,3, 196–215) which shows how each of the characters has experienced it. Alsemero introduces these reflections with an appropriate image: 'What an opacous body had that moon / That last chang'd on us' (V,3,196–7). Not only is the moon symbolic of change: it was thought to affect those mutable creatures, lovers and madmen. Alsemero's image thus draws together three of the play's themes: desire, change and madness.

Imagery

There is another image, also associated with the unsettling quality of desire, which appears in this first scene: the image of poison. Alsemero's lines about the hidden malady (line 24) hint at it first; then he and Beatrice take it up in a curious discussion (I,1,109–30) followed by a kind of comic echo in Diaphanta's exchange with Jasperino. The noble lovers discuss the doctrine that 'one man's meat is another man's poison'. The stress is on the irrationality and power of taste; points which obviously reflect on the irrationality and power of love. The moral point about this discussion is the equation it implicitly makes between taste and love, and the dangerous consequences of such an equation. Beatrice's fault lies in treating men as though they were as expendable as cherries. So the extensive development of their speeches alerts us to the topic's importance in the play.

But this is only a beginning: the whole subject of poison and antidote, sickness and cure, resounds through the play. As Alsemero and Beatrice talk, Diaphanta tells Jasperino she has a cure for his 'madness', i.e. his desire, in a brief scene that anticipates the antics of the false madmen in Alibius's asylum. Later, Beatrice refers to De Flores as a 'serpent' (line 225), i.e. a poisonous snake, and this image too recurs. In II,2, Beatrice says that Alsemero's kiss '. . . has an enemy, a hateful one, / That wishes poison to't . . .' (16–17), a most unfair reflection on Alonzo, who knows nothing of her treachery. The point is, of course, that *she* wishes poison to *him*; this is a kind of long-range transferred epithet. Later in the same scene, Beatrice flatters De Flores by supposing he has been treated by a good physician (line 73) so improved is his appearance. So when, in IV,2, Alsemero says of De Flores that the sight of him is poison for Beatrice (line 98), we can savour the dramatic irony. And this irony deepens even further when Beatrice herself, filled with admiration at De Flores's resourcefulness, exclaims in V,1,70–71 that 'His face loathes one, / But look upon his care, who would not love him?'

Beatrice began the play by falling for Alsemero because of his beauty and concluding that he also had a good character (III,2,6–14) but she ends it by contrasting De Flores's vile face with his deeds. Yet his deeds are, of course, as vile as his face. Beatrice's failure to see this provides an eloquent illustration of her character and her predicament, in a complex development of the poison/antidote image. Alsemero seems to be the 'cure' for the 'poison' of Alonzo, but De Flores is required as an 'antidote'. Then De Flores in turn becomes a kind of poison which Beatrice comes to want: he is both poison and cure. Traditionally, sex has been represented paradoxically as poison and cure: it creates a need and satisfies it. So it is quite appropriate that a play preoccupied with sexual relations should have such a paradoxical image at its heart as the poison/antidote one. Even the curious episode of the virgin-testing potion relates to it, for the same potion produces opposite effects according to the state of the girl who takes it. Beatrice is able to feign the right symptoms, and Diaphanta dies as a result. Yet Diaphanta's death helps, in the end, to betray Beatrice: Alsemero's potion is both a 'guarantee' of Beatrice's innocence, yet another step towards her downfall.

The full significance of the poison image becomes apparent at two points in Act V. In the second scene Tomazo suddenly takes a violent aversion to De Flores. The man's face is so horrible, it flatly contradicts the notion that he could be 'honest' as people say. And Tomazo finds, 'a contrariety in nature / Betwixt that face and me ...' (V,2,13–14). He imagines De Flores as being so poisonous that even a sword in contact with him would be permanently tainted. In Scene 3 Beatrice confesses to complicity in the murder of Alonzo, exclaiming that in employing De Flores she has 'kiss'd poison for't, strok'd a serpent' (V,3,66). The disturbing sensuality of her words, and the contradictions they embody – kissing poison and stroking serpents are the last things one would normally do – echo the violence of Tomazo's reaction, and his perception of the contradiction between De Flores's reputed honesty and the horror of his appearance. Here the poison image and the appearance/reality image fuse to suggest the way in which the whole moral order has been turned upside down.

Moral chaos is also represented in a third major image, closely associated with the others, i.e. the image of madness, both inside the asylum and outside it. There is a sense in which both De Flores and Beatrice are 'mad' because they ignore all the laws and conventions 'sane' people conform to: this sort of madness is equivalent to the unfettered working of the will. Beatrice knows no restraints: she reaches for what she wants and employs any means to get it. De Flores has little to lose but life: he does the same. The violence and horror of the main action constitute a far worse madness than the gentle horseplay of the asylum, with its simpletons and crazed poets. Desire itself is a kind of madness, which blinds its victims – Alonzo, Alsemero, Diaphanta. Although Franciscus and Antonio only pretend to be mad, they really are while they are possessed by desire for Isabella; they are also fools. Isabella brings this point vividly home to Antonio at IV,3,130: and her use of disguise to do it makes a link between the madness theme and other images important in the play – not least the contradiction between appearance and reality.

This contradiction is an obsessive theme in the period. It pervades Shakespeare's tragedies, Jonson's comedies and almost every other major play. Such a preoccupation is characteristic in an age of extreme instability such as the early 17th century in Europe, when religious wars and political upheavals were endemic. Actual death and prophecies of doom were everywhere to be found, given greater currency than ever before by the increasing activities of the printing presses and slowly improving communications. Finding many different kinds of expression, this theme produces in the period's drama a fascination with intrigue, plotting, secrecy, deception and all the violence that ensues from such things. Sexual desire becomes symbolic of general treachery, the unpredictability of life and its dangers. Jacobean tragedy is invariably lecherous, bloody and violent – sometimes gratuitously, for sensational effect – often because these qualities correspond to the deeper truths of life the dramatists wished to express. More often still, a combination of both sensationalism and truth. Central to their perceptions was the feeling that the life of the body is a misleading puzzle, a compelling road to disaster or a bad joke.

Though many dramatists appear to have had doubts about the validity of conventional Christian doctrine, they were nevertheless sufficiently imbued with it to give them an acute sense of disgust with the physical when compared with the spiritual. Their philosophy was that even if Heaven and Hell do not exist, they serve as excellent metaphors for describing this life. Human existence is a thing of appearances either way: if Heaven and Hell are real, they are more important than life before death; if not, there is nothing left to hang on to but power, gratification and the art of survival. Death is the ultimate puzzle that brings the meaning of life into doubt – and of death these dramatists were continually and acutely aware.

Primarily associated with the appearance/reality theme are Beatrice and De Flores. Beatrice's looks belie her behaviour, while De Flores's inferior role for a while saves him from detection. Appropriately, the two are truly known to each other, though not to anyone else. But while De Flores understands his own nature from the start, Beatrice is a fascinating case of self-deception; and the play traces her descent from wilful innocence to full complicity in evil. Until the last possible moment she appears innocent to herself. Only then is she aware of her true identity. This motif is echoed in the behaviour of Antonio and Franciscus, who only come to themselves when they receive salutary shocks. The same is true, to a lesser degree, of Alibius and Vermandero, who both learn unpalatable truths about their own blindness. The image of eyesight, which is naturally associated with the appearance/reality theme, is in evidence here, as it is throughout the play. What people think they see is often something quite different: the eyes should reveal the truth, but are deceivers. Isabella makes this point ironically when she tricks Antonio: 'You a quick-sighted lover! Come not near me!' (IV,3,133), but the point is made implicitly over and over again in the play: if normal eyesight is defective, love makes us completely blind. Thus love too becomes a matter of appearances: Alsemero, Alonzo and De Flores all love Beatrice's beauty; they know little of her. Beatrice rejects Alonzo for Alsemero when she knows nothing about him but his looks. Vermandero goes by appearances; Alonzo is betrayed by them. So, in a way, is De Flores, unsurprised though he is by the catastrophe. For De Flores fails to 'see' the ghost (V,1,57), dismissing it as 'a mist of conscience' – a telling phrase that describes his state by the end of the play. Even his acute vision is clouded by a mist of desire and remorse. Confession becomes almost a relief in the final scene, which makes it come easily and then defiantly.

General questions

1 In what ways is the first scene of the play important?

Suggested notes for essay

Conveyance of information; characters and their relationships; places, times, social circumstances. Establishment of plot mechanism. Themes. Imagery. The major figures of the main plot – Alsemero, Beatrice, De Flores – are all presented in their primary relationships: Alsemero and Beatrice in love, and De Flores adoring Beatrice. Their characteristics are sketched in: Alsemero's change from indifference to women, to love; Beatrice's changeability, De Flores's obsessive desire. Minor figures also appear: Jasperino, Diaphanta, Vermandero. Their characters also made clear – and their roles. Following from this, the plot mechanism of change: Beatrice changing from Alonzo to Alsemero; Alsemero changing from indifference to women, to love. Beatrice's father shown to be firmly in favour of a marriage she opposes. Jasperino and Diaphanta paralleling relationship of Beatrice and Alsemero.

Themes: desire, and the change it promotes; the subordination of women, the conflict of desire with order and convention.

Imagery: change, poison and medicine all important for supporting the themes.

Finally: questions of tone and style. Sinewy, rapid movement established very quickly. This could be the opening of a comedy but for various signs in the imagery: fire, change, desire etc.

2 Discuss the importance of sexual desire as a motivating force in the play.

3 What do you understand by the term 'Domestic Tragedy', and what relevance does it have for *The Changeling*?

4 Examine the way in which the play uses contrast and comparison of pairs of characters.

5 Give a detailed account of the way in which the relationship between Beatrice and De Flores is presented.

6 What relationship is there between the main plot and the sub-plot?

7 What kinds of comedy occur in the play and how important are they?

8 In what ways is knowledge of the social position of women in the seventeenth century significant for understanding *The Changeling*?

9 What are the major images used in the play and how do they relate to one another?

10 What elements of spectacle does the play utilize and to what effect?

Further reading

N. W. Bawcutt: ed. *The Changeling* (Methuen, 1958). This is the best edition of the play, with a judicious and concise introduction.

M. C. Bradbrook: *Themes and Conventions of Elizabethan Tragedy* (CUP, 1960). First published in 1935, this remains a standard guide to the period. There is a good chapter on Middleton.

F. T. Bowers: *Elizabethan Revenge Tragedy* (Princeton, 1940). A useful book for putting *The Changeling* in the context of dramatic history.

U. Ellis-Fermor: *The Jacobean Drama* (Methuen, 1936). A more detailed study than Bowers, with a very sympathetic section on *The Changeling*. Ellis-Fermor also gives a helpful updated bibliography in the later editions.

J. R. Mulryne: *Thomas Middleton* (Longman, 1979). A brief recent study with useful commentary on *The Changeling*. Rowley has yet to find such consideration.

Pan study aids Titles published in the Brodie's Notes series

W. H. Auden Selected Poetry

Jane Austen Emma Mansfield Park Northanger Abbey Persuasion
Pride and Prejudice

Anthologies of Poetry Ten Twentieth Century Poets The Poet's Tale
The Metaphysical Poets

Samuel Beckett Waiting for Godot

Arnold Bennett The Old Wives' Tale

William Blake Songs of Innocence and Experience

Robert Bolt A Man for All Seasons

Harold Brighouse Hobson's Choice

Charlotte Brontë Jane Eyre

Emily Brontë Wuthering Heights

Robert Browning Selected Poetry

John Bunyan The Pilgrim's Progress

Geoffrey Chaucer (parallel texts editions) The Franklin's Tale
The Knight's Tale The Miller's Tale The Nun's Priest's Tale
The Pardoner's Tale Prologue to the Canterbury Tales
The Wife of Bath's Tale

Richard Church Over the Bridge

John Clare Selected Poetry and Prose

Samuel Taylor Coleridge Selected Poetry and Prose

Wilkie Collins The Woman in White

William Congreve The Way of the World

Joseph Conrad The Nigger of the Narcissus & Youth
The Secret Agent

Charles Dickens Bleak House David Copperfield Dombey and Son
Great Expectations Hard Times Little Dorrit Oliver Twist
Our Mutual Friend A Tale of Two Cities

Gerald Durrell My Family and Other Animals

George Eliot Middlemarch The Mill on the Floss Silas Marner

T. S. Eliot Murder in the Cathedral Selected Poems

J. G. Farrell The Siege of Krishnapur

Henry Fielding Joseph Andrews

F. Scott Fitzgerald The Great Gatsby

E. M. Forster Howards End A Passage to India
Where Angels Fear to Tread

William Golding Lord of the Flies The Spire

Oliver Goldsmith Two Plays of Goldsmith: She Stoops to Conquer;
The Good Natured Man

Graham Greene Brighton Rock The Power and the Glory
The Quiet American

Thom Gunn and Ted Hughes Selected Poems

Thomas Hardy Chosen Poems of Thomas Hardy
Far from the Madding Crowd Jude the Obscure
The Mayor of Casterbridge Return of the Native
Tess of the d'Urbervilles The Trumpet-Major

L. P. Hartley The Go-Between The Shrimp and the Anemone

Joseph Heller Catch-22

Ernest Hemingway For Whom the Bell Tolls
The Old Man and the Sea

Barry Hines A Kestrel for a Knave

Gerard Manley Hopkins Poetry and Prose of Gerard Manley Hopkins

Aldous Huxley Brave New World

Henry James Washington Square

Ben Jonson The Alchemist Volpone

James Joyce A Portrait of the Artist as a Young Man Dubliners

John Keats Selected Poems and Letters of John Keats

Ken Kesey One Flew over the Cuckoo's Nest

Rudyard Kipling Kim

D. H. Lawrence The Rainbow Selected Tales Sons and Lovers

Harper Lee To Kill a Mockingbird

Laurie Lee As I Walked out One Midsummer Morning
Cider with Rosie

Thomas Mann Death in Venice & Tonio Kröger
Christopher Marlowe Doctor Faustus Edward the Second

W. Somerset Maugham Of Human Bondage

Gavin Maxwell Ring of Bright Water

Arthur Miller The Crucible Death of a Salesman

John Milton A Choice of Milton's Verse Comus and Samson Agonistes Paradise Lost I, II

Sean O'Casey Juno and the Paycock
The Shadow of a Gunman and the Plough and the Stars

George Orwell Animal Farm 1984

John Osborne Luther

Alexander Pope Selected Poetry

J. B. Priestley An Inspector Calls

Siegfried Sassoon Memoirs of a Fox-Hunting Man

Peter Shaffer The Royal Hunt of the Sun

William Shakespeare Antony and Cleopatra As You Like It
Coriolanus Hamlet Henry IV (Part I) Henry IV (Part II) Henry V
Julius Caesar King Lear Love's Labour's Lost Macbeth Measure for
Measure The Merchant of Venice A Midsummer Night's Dream
Much Ado about Nothing Othello Richard II Richard III Romeo and
Juliet The Sonnets The Taming of the Shrew The Tempest Twelfth
Night The Winter's Tale

G. B. Shaw Androcles and the Lion Arms and the Man
Caesar and Cleopatra The Doctor's Dilemma Pygmalion Saint Joan

Richard Sheridan Plays of Sheridan: The Rivals; The Critic;
The School for Scandal

John Steinbeck The Grapes of Wrath Of Mice and Men & The Pearl

Tom Stoppard Rosencrantz and Guildenstern are Dead

J. M. Synge The Playboy of the Western World

Jonathan Swift Gulliver's Travels

Alfred Tennyson Selected Poetry

William Thackeray Vanity Fair

Flora Thompson Lark Rise to Candleford

Dylan Thomas Under Milk Wood

Anthony Trollope Barchester Towers

Mark Twain Huckleberry Finn

Keith Waterhouse Billy Liar

Evelyn Waugh Decline and Fall Scoop

John Webster The Duchess of Malfi The White Devil

H. G. Wells The History of Mr Polly The War of the Worlds

Oscar Wilde The Importance of Being Earnest

Virginia Woolf To the Lighthouse

William Wordsworth The Prelude (Books 1, 2)

William Wycherley The Country Wife

John Wyndham The Chrysalids

W. B. Yeats Selected Poetry

Pan study aids

Published jointly by Heinemann Educational Books and Pan Books

Pan Study Aids is a major new series developed to help school and college students prepare for examinations. All the authors are experienced teachers/examiners at O level, School Certificate and equivalent examinations and authors of textbooks used in schools and colleges worldwide

Each volume in the series:
- explains its subject and covers clearly and concisely and with excellent illustrations the essential points of the syllabus, drawing attention to common areas of difficulty and to areas which carry most marks in the exam

- gives guidance on how to plan revision, and prepare for the exam, outlining what examiners are looking for

- provides practice by including typical exam questions and exercises

Titles available: Physics, Chemistry, Maths, Human Biology, English Language, Geography 1 & 2, Economics, Commerce, Accounts and Book-keeping, British Government and Politics, History 1 & 2, Effective Study Skills, French, German, Spanish, Sociology

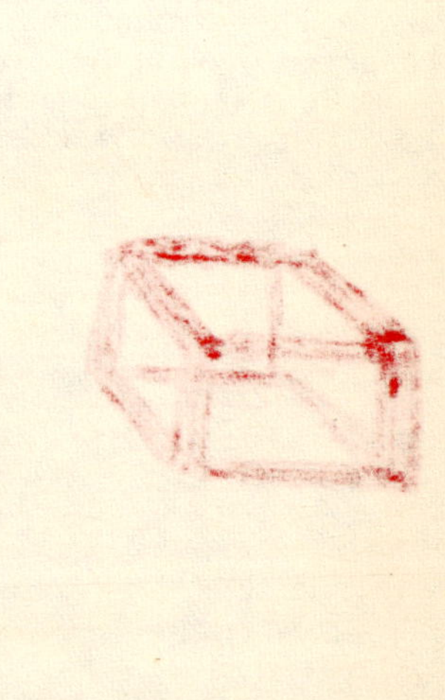